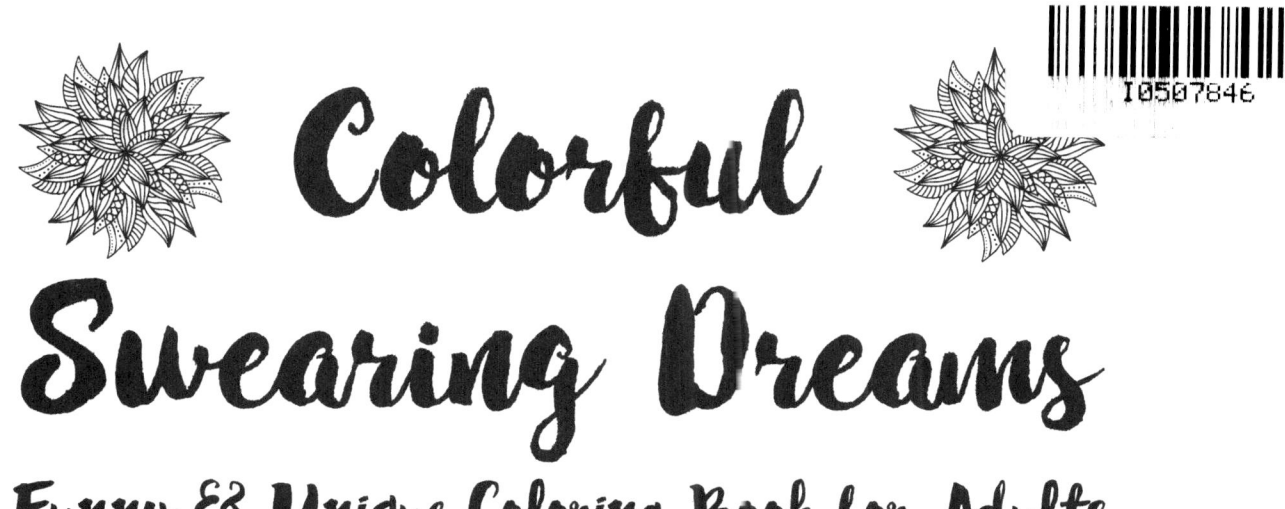

Colorful Swearing Dreams
Funny & Unique Coloring Book for Adults

IS YOUR STRESS LEVEL HIGH?
THIS BOOK WILL KICK YOUR STRESS AWAY!

Multiple studies revealed that coloring mandalas, geometric patterns & other shapes helps reduce stress and anxiety for adults.

This book contains 30 pages of beautiful & intricate designs mixed up with funny cats and dogs facing each other by using their most powerful and smelliest farts in a vicious fight.
Anyone who loves cats and dogs knows how awful theirs farts can smell!
The concept of this book is to imagine what would happen if we let cats and dogs fight with their farts!

This really quirky and off-color coloring book is ideal for anyone who loves cats, dogs, pets or anyone with a sense of humor, to be honest!

Each page is single-sided for getting the best coloring experience.

TIME TO COLOR THE STRESS AWAY!

All Rights Reserved. Colorful Swearing Dreams

No part of this book may be reproduced, stored in a retrieval system, or transmitted in any form or by any means, electronic, mechanical, photocopying, recording, or otherwise, without the prior written permission of the author.

Colorful Swearing Dreams

Swear Word Coloring Book for Adults

Coloring Test Page

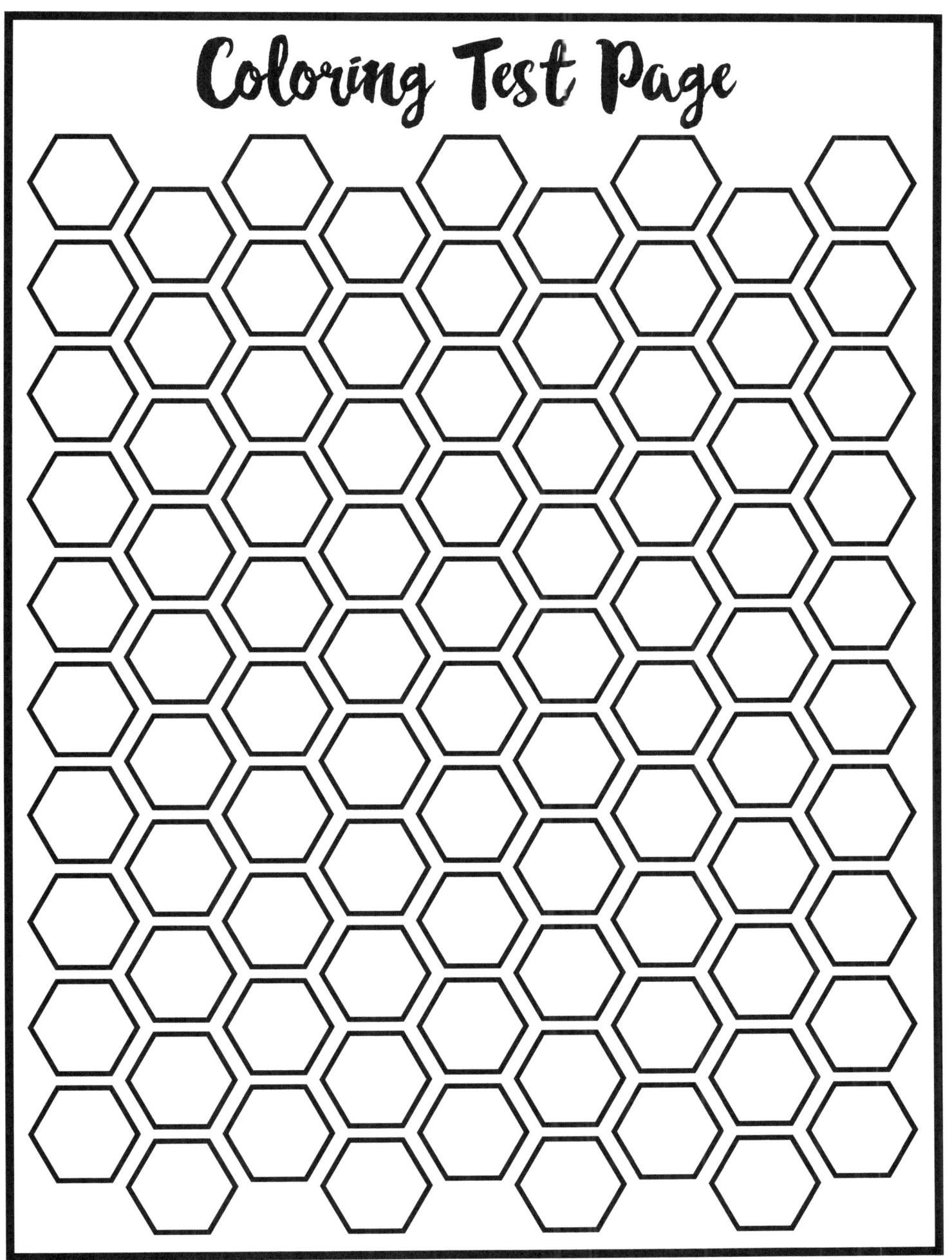

Colorful Swearing Dreams

Swear Word Coloring Book for Adults

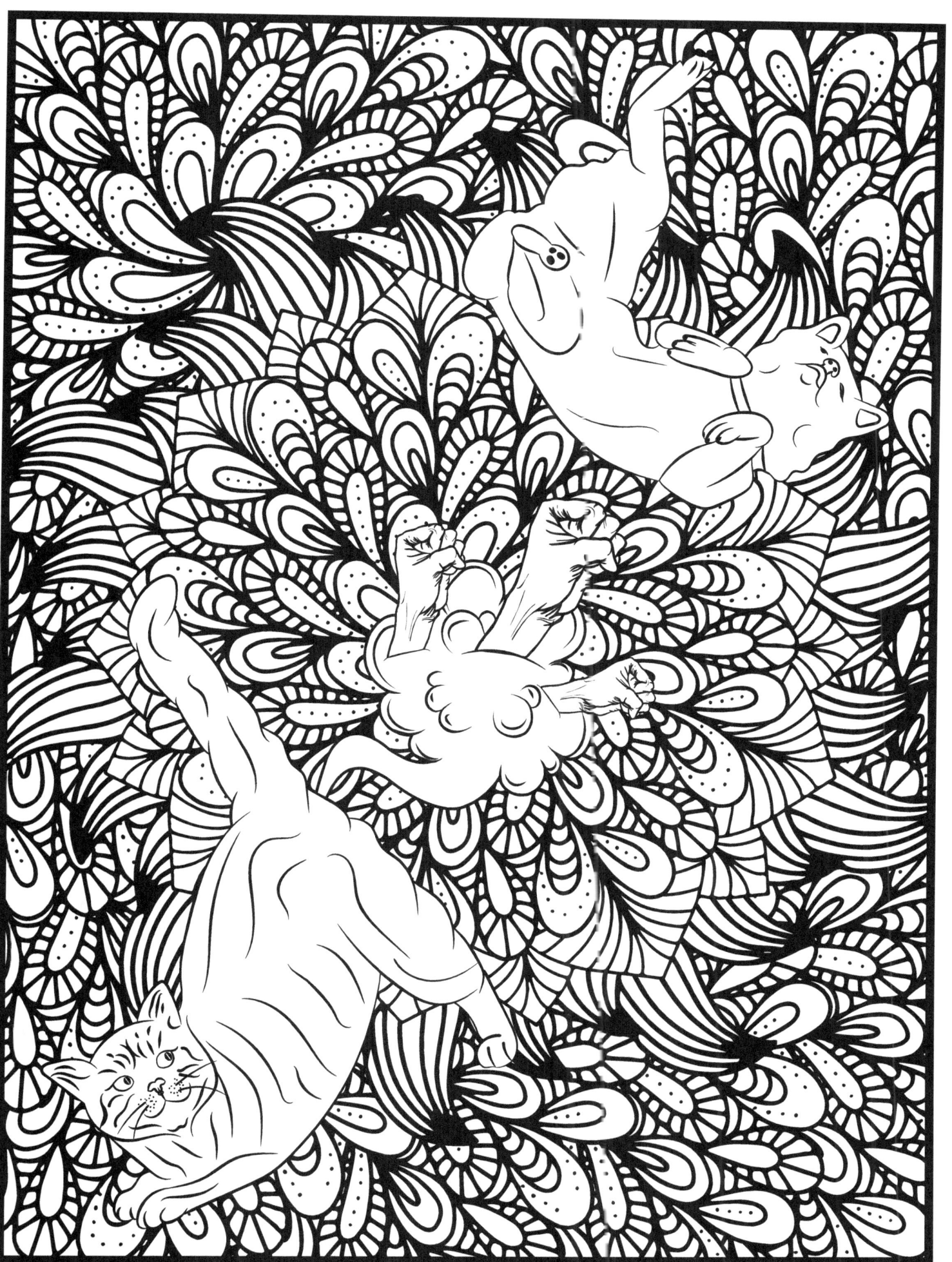

Colorful Swearing Dreams

Swear Word Coloring Book for Adults

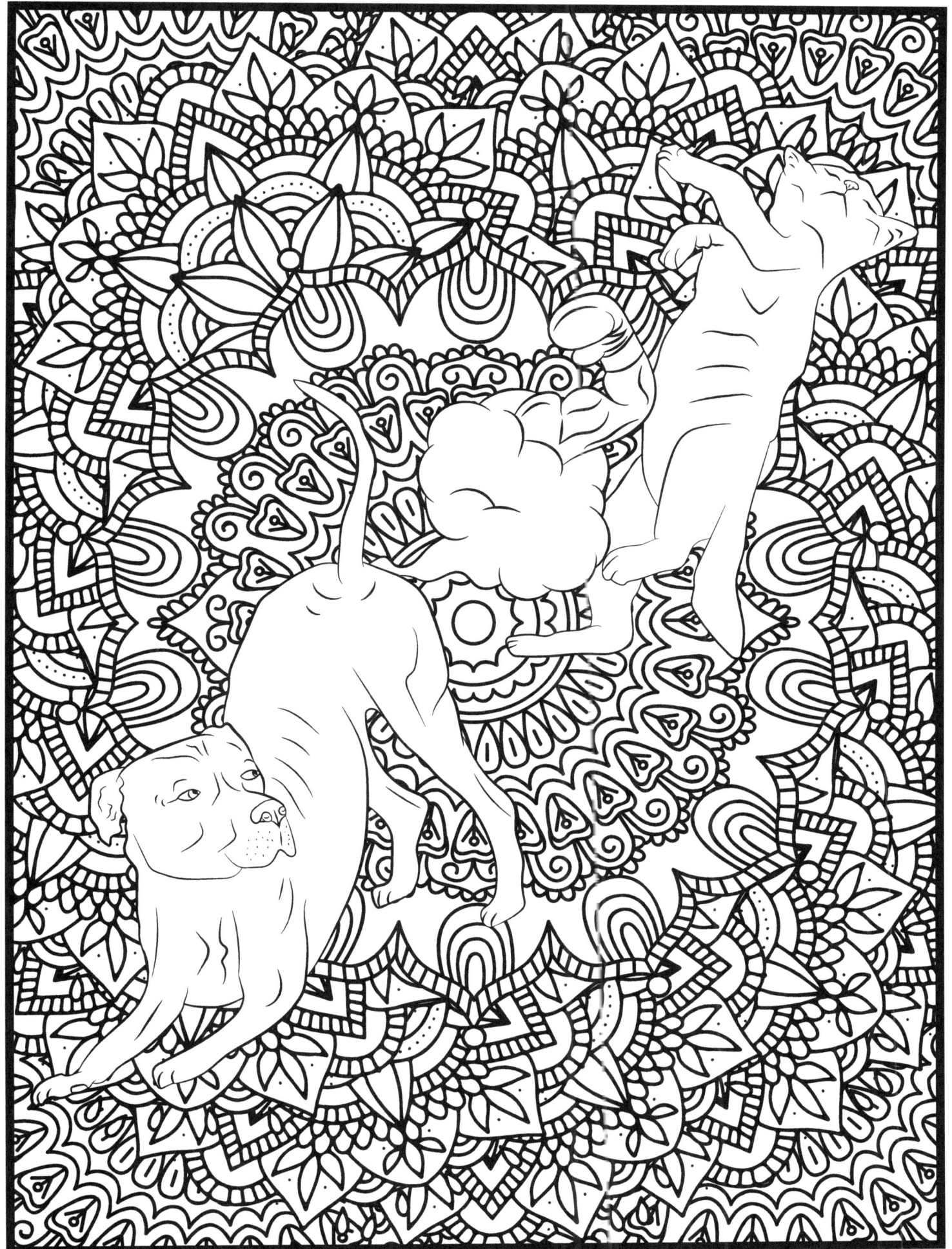

Colorful Swearing Dreams

Swear Word Coloring Book for Adults

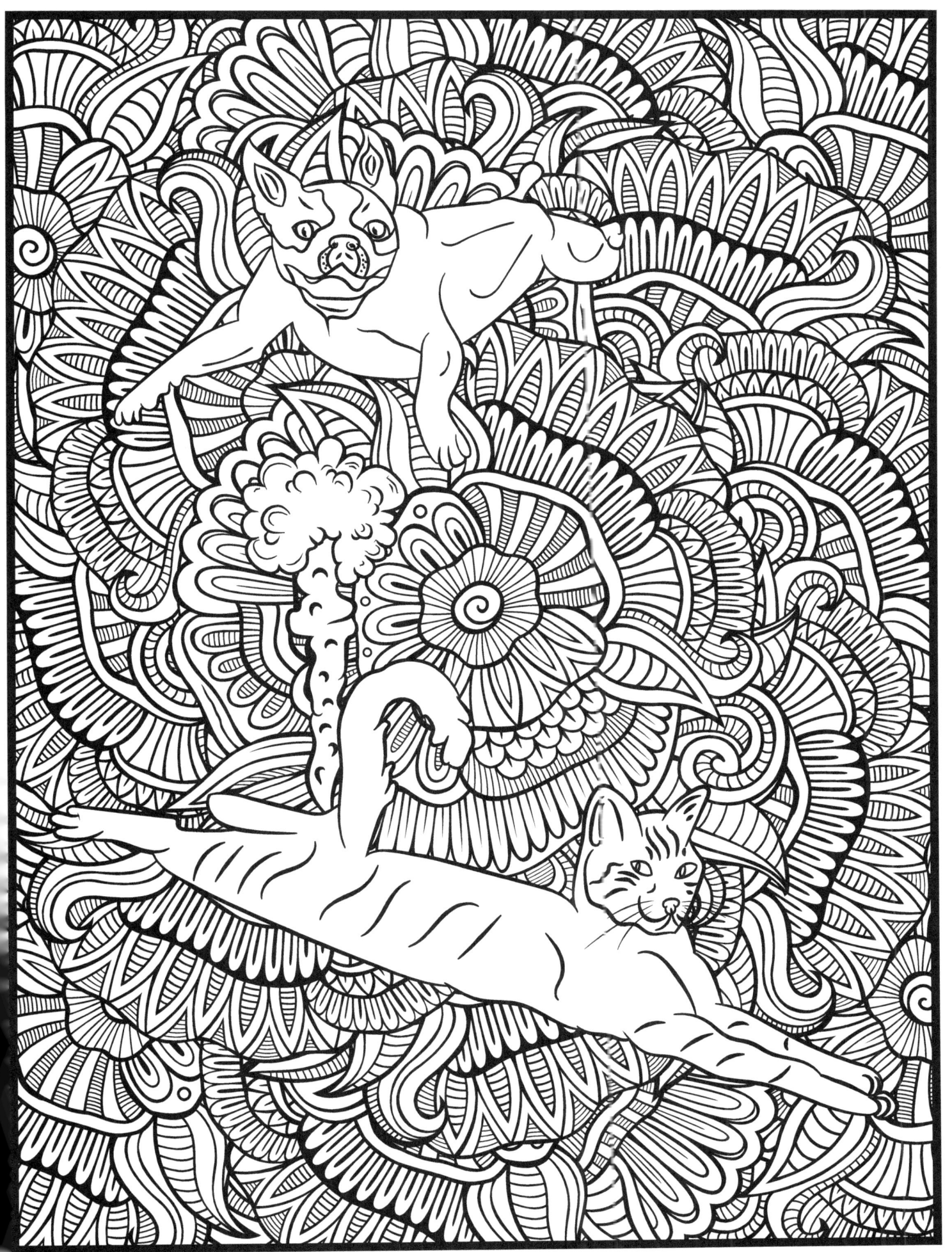

Colorful Swearing Dreams

Swear Word Coloring Book for Adults

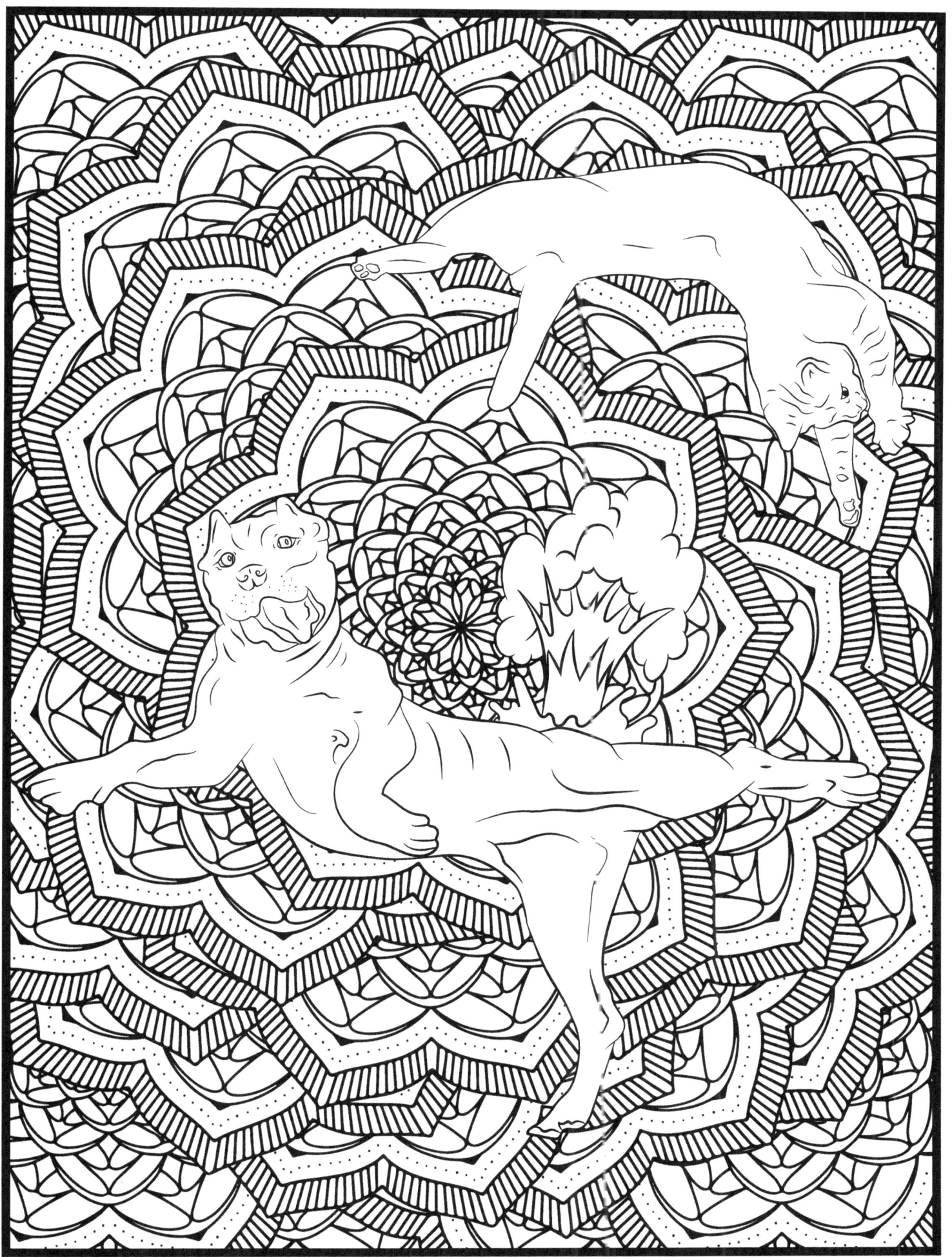

Colorful Swearing Dreams

Swear Word Coloring Book for Adults

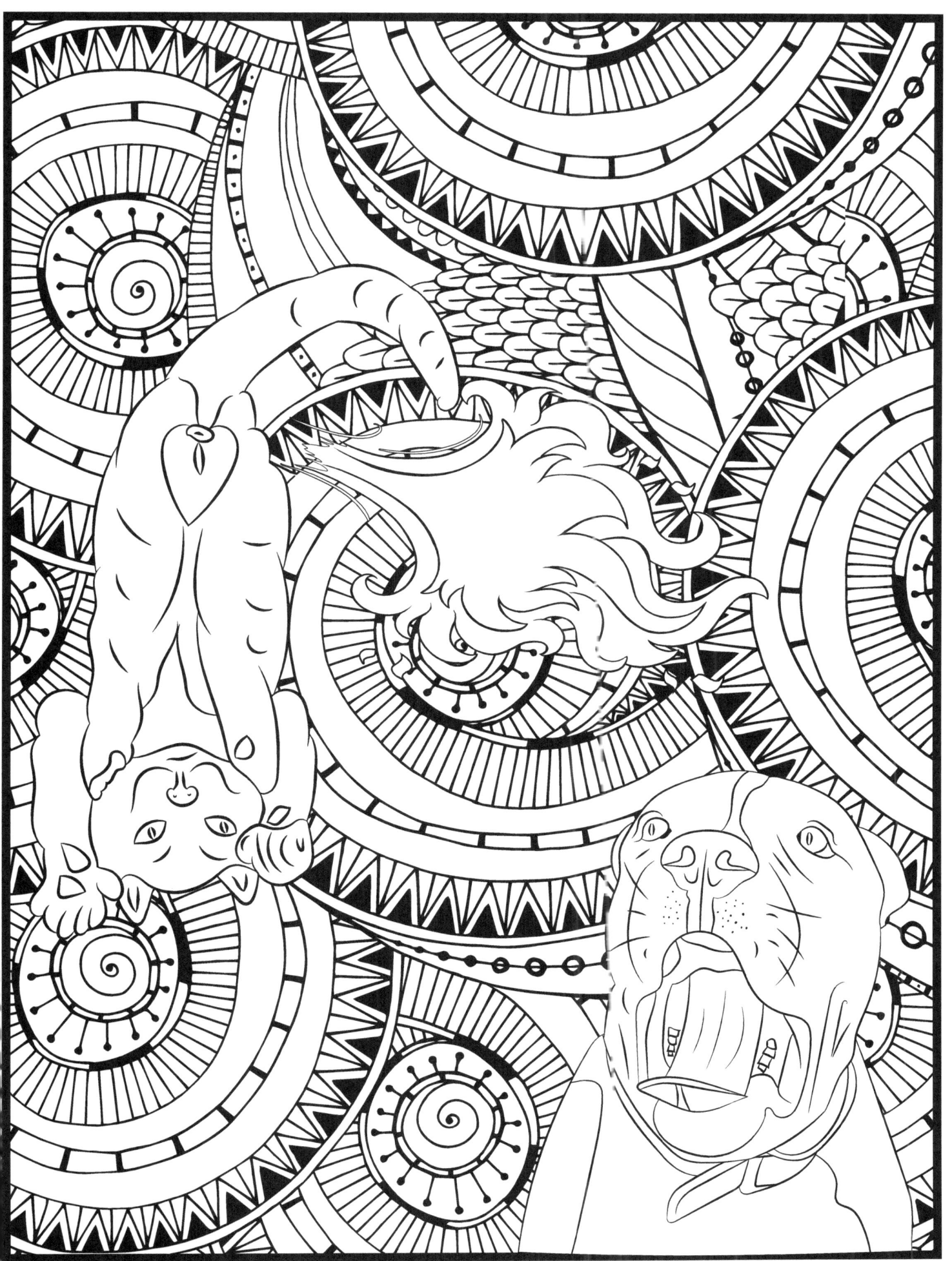

Colorful Sweering Dreams

Swear Word Coloring Book for Adults

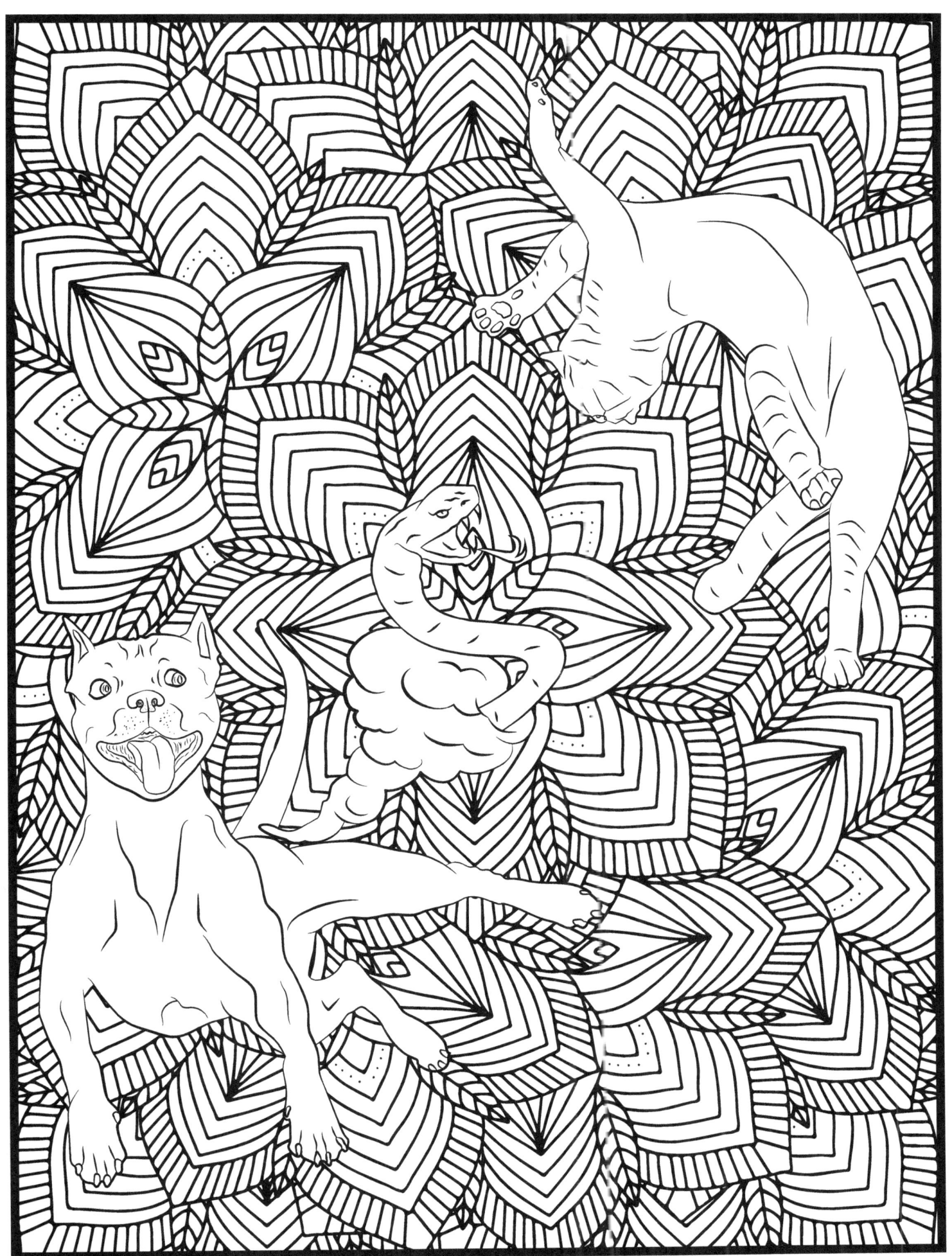

Colorful Swearing Dreams

Swear Words Coloring Book for Adults

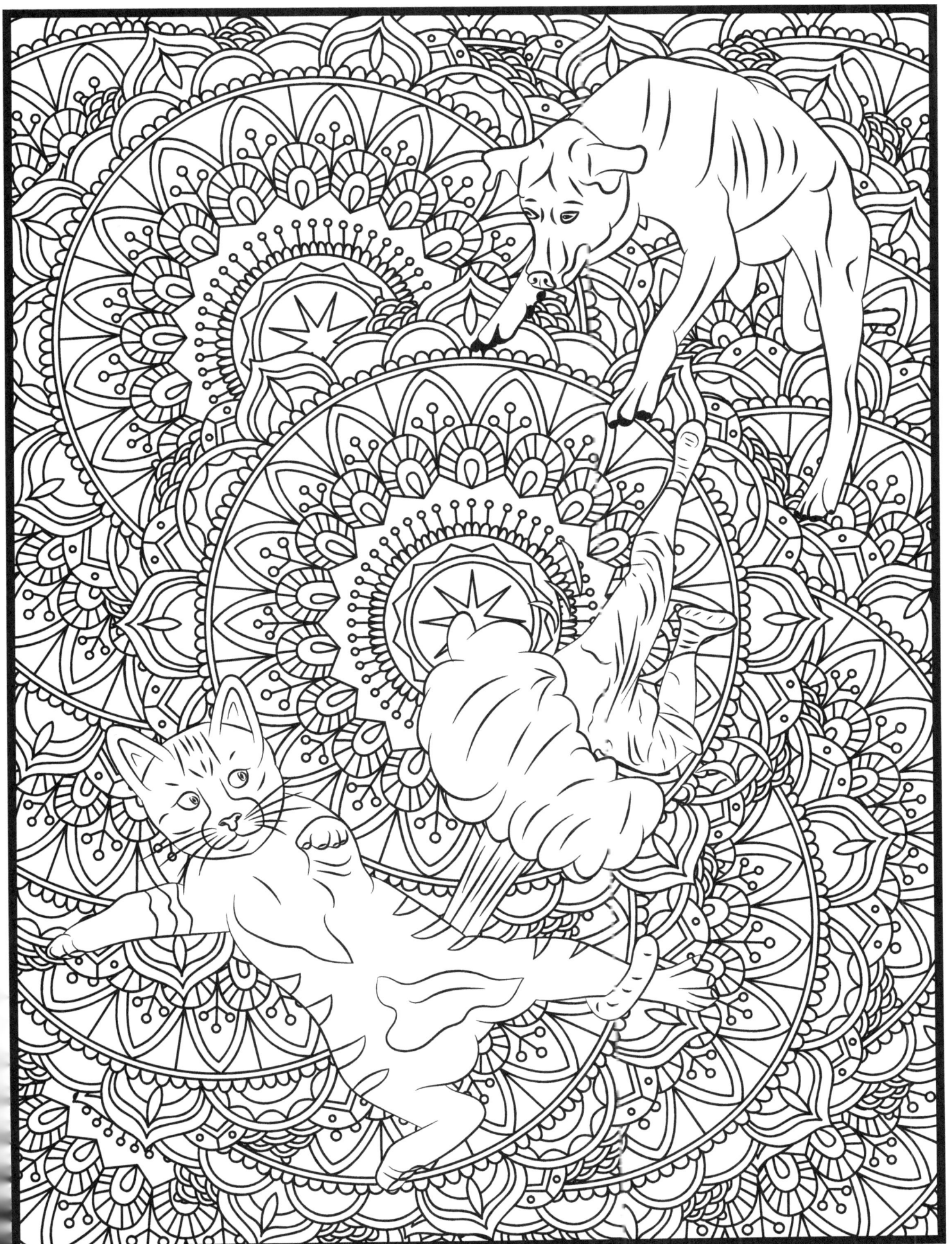

Colorful Swearing Dreams

Swear Word Coloring Book for Adults

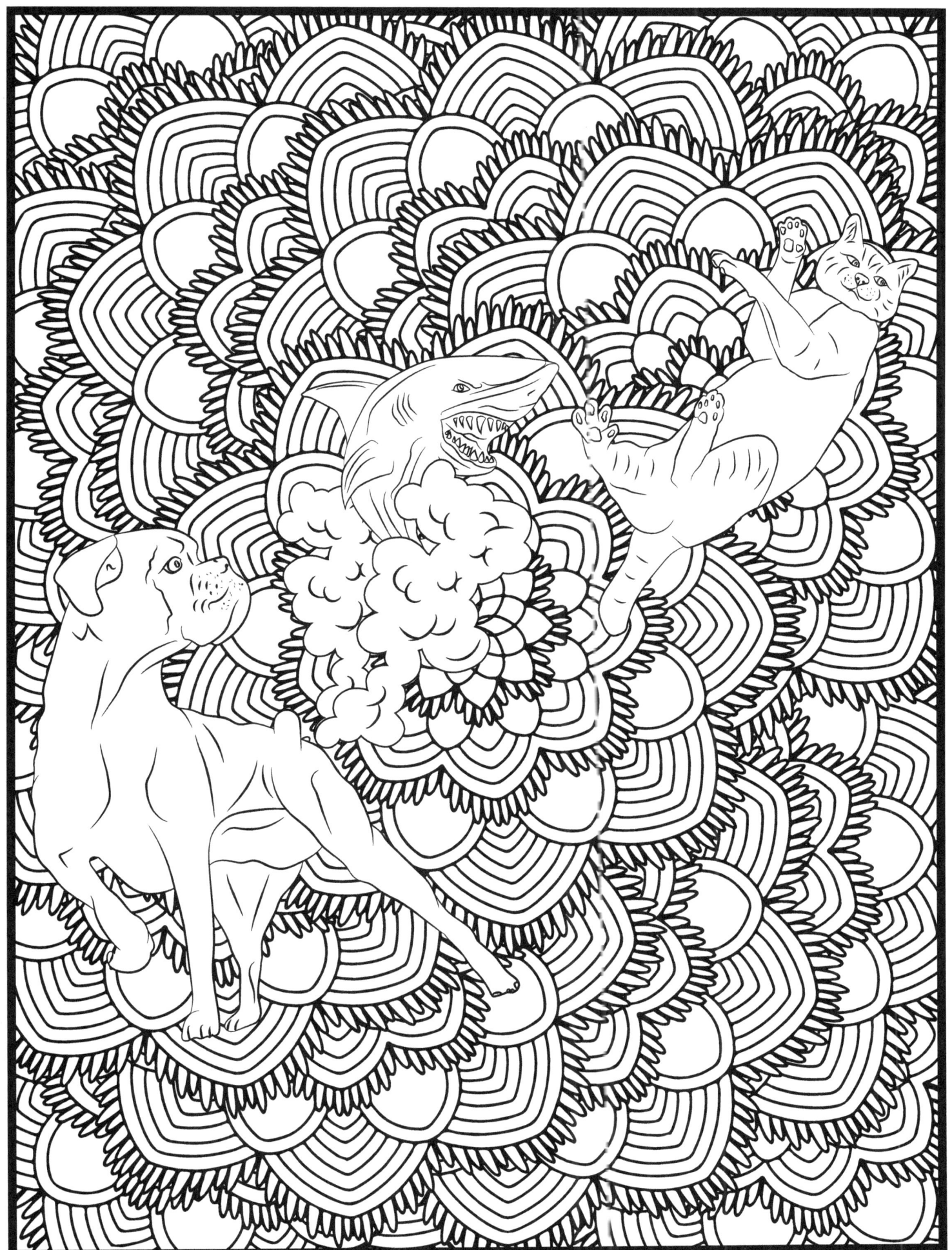

Colorful Swearing Dreams

Swear Word Coloring Book for Adults

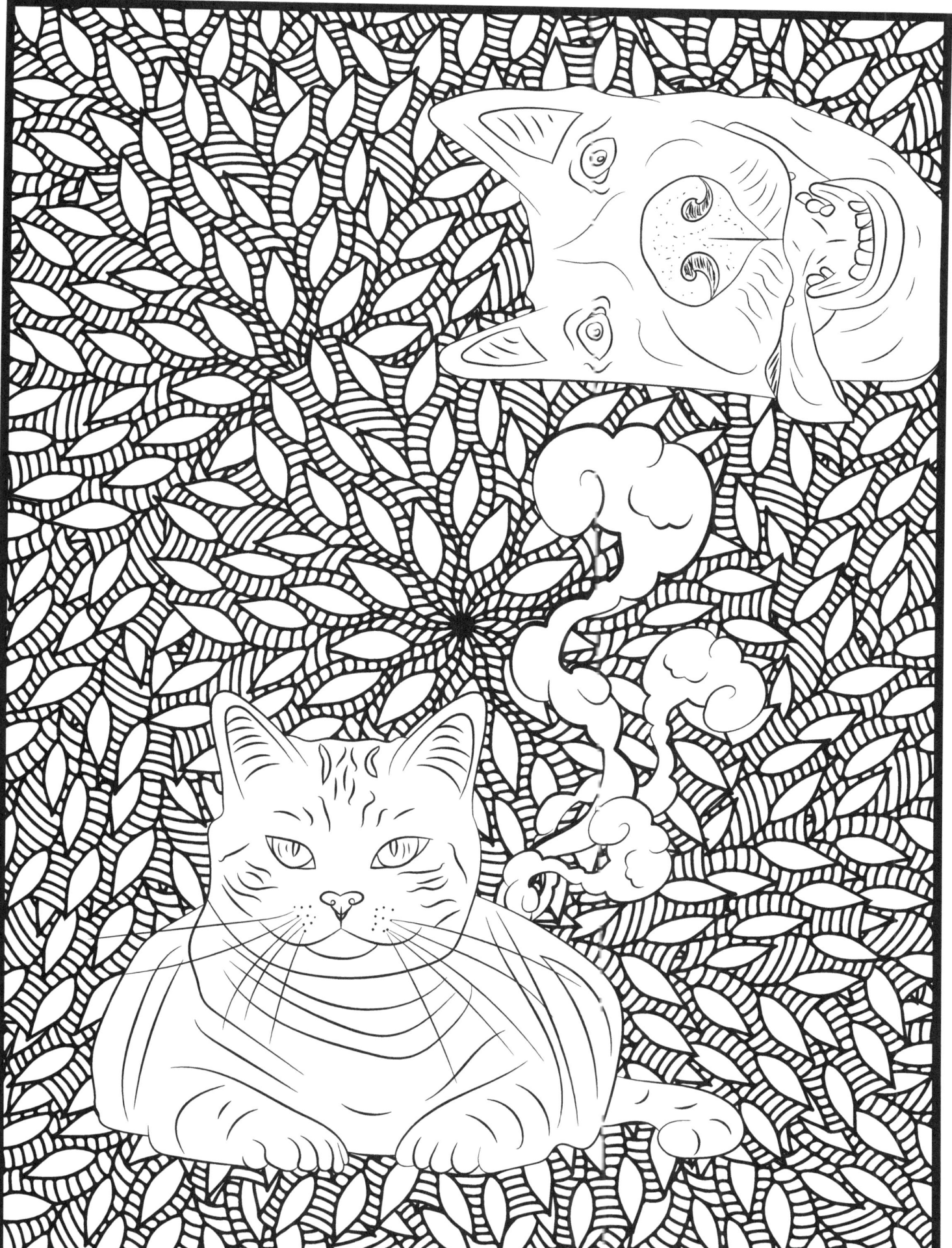

Colorful Swearing Dreams

Swear Word Coloring Book for Adults

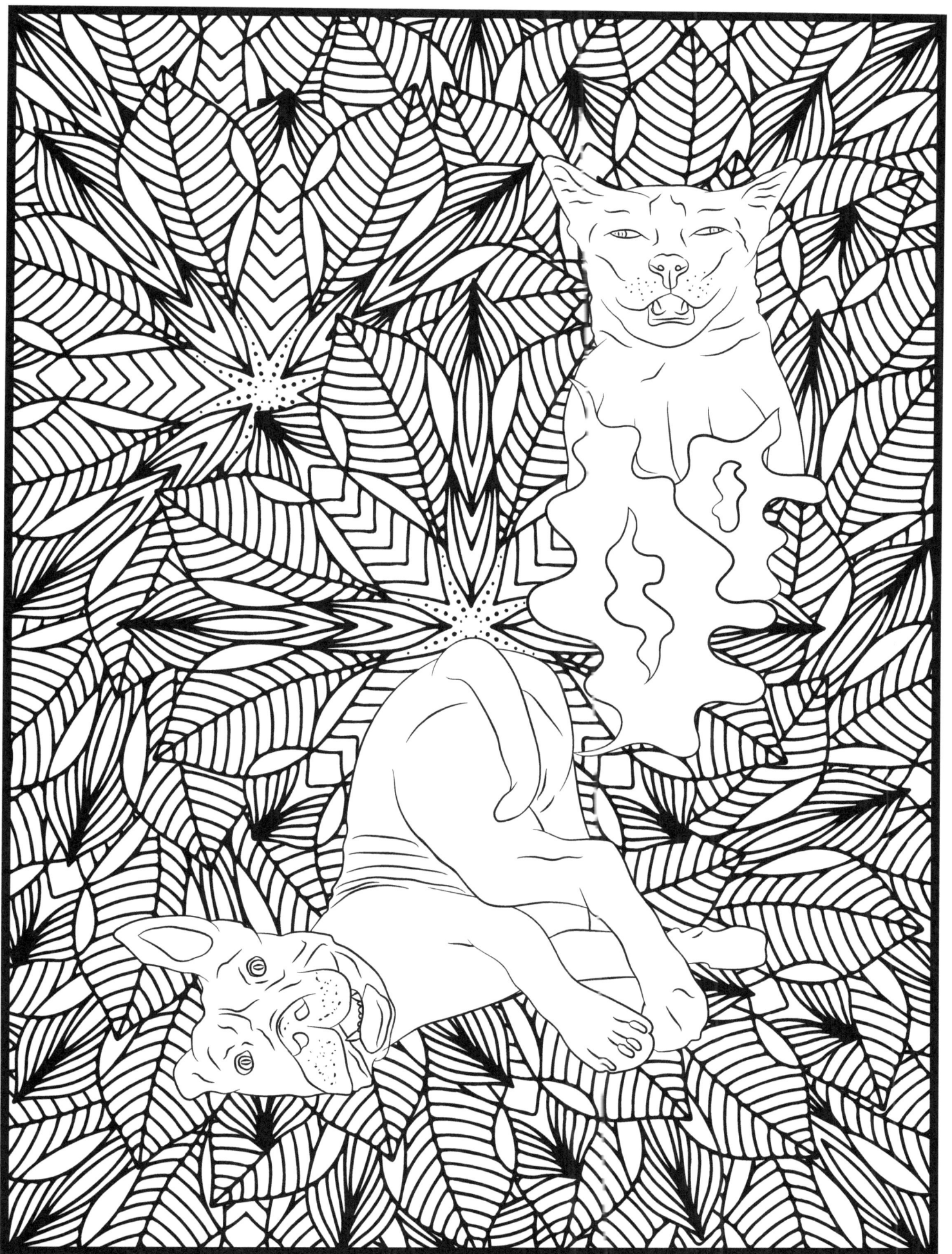

Colorful Swearing Dreams

Swear Word Coloring Book for Adults

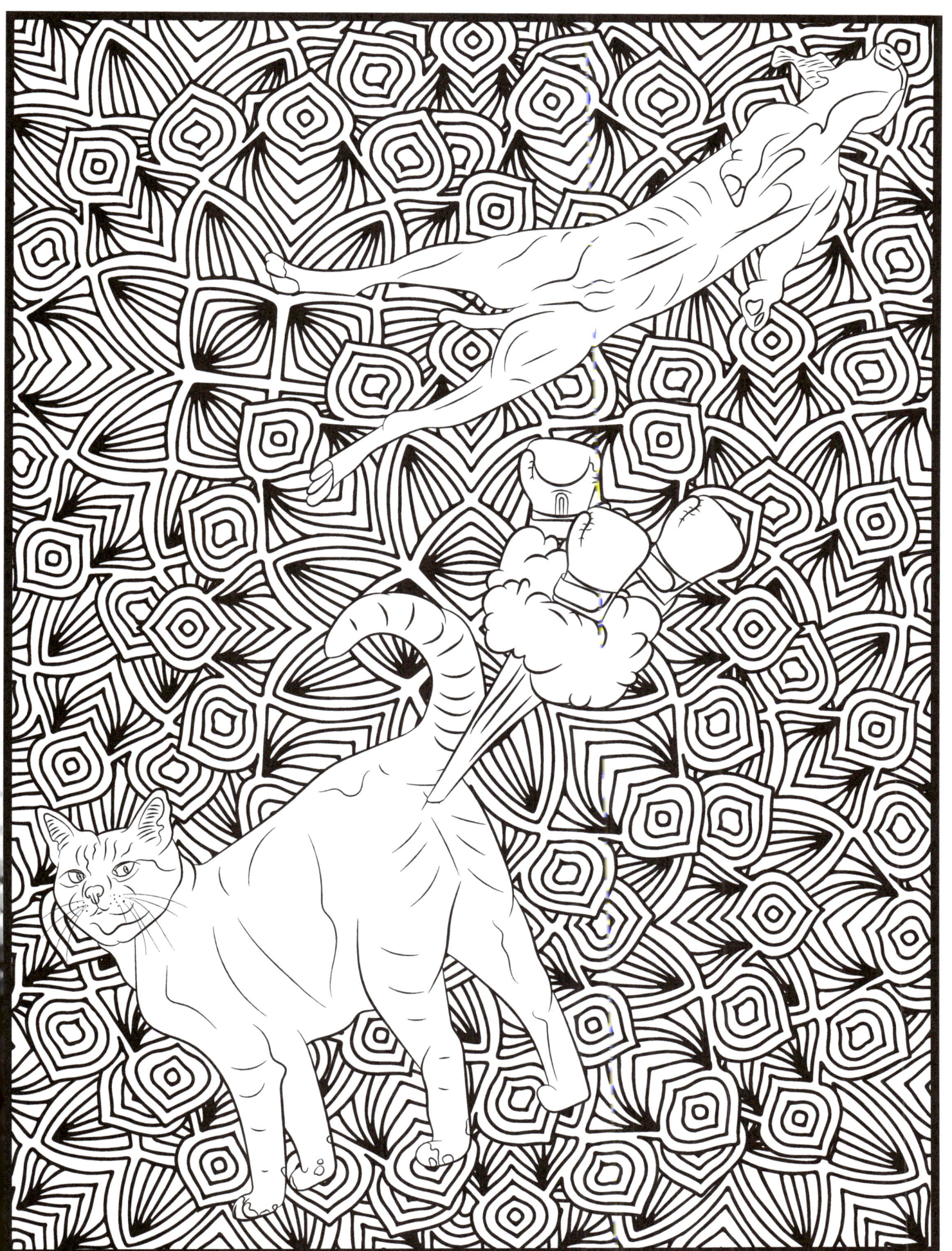

Colorful Swearing Dreams

Sweet Word Coloring Book for Adults

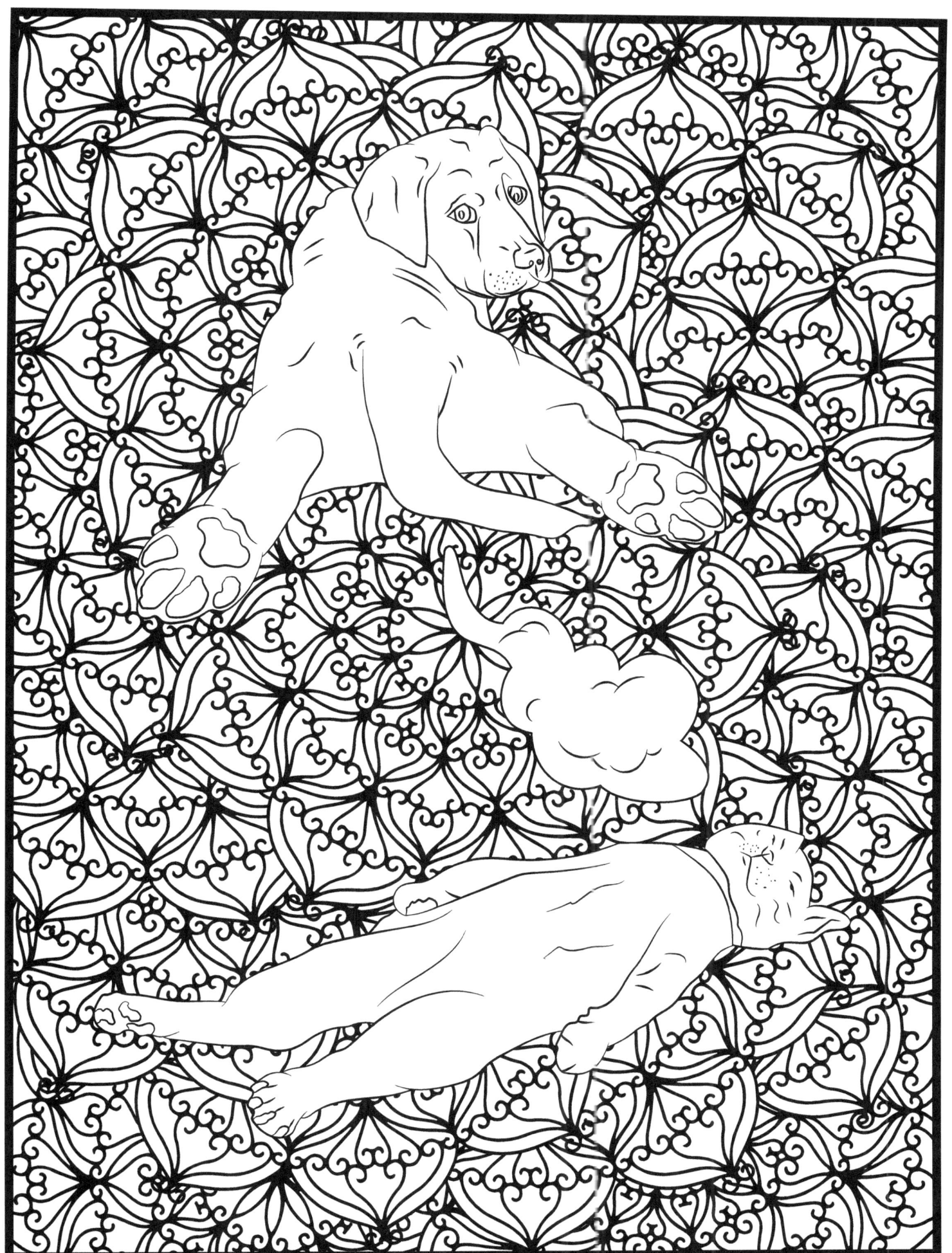

Colorful Swearing Dreams

Swear Word Coloring Book for Adults

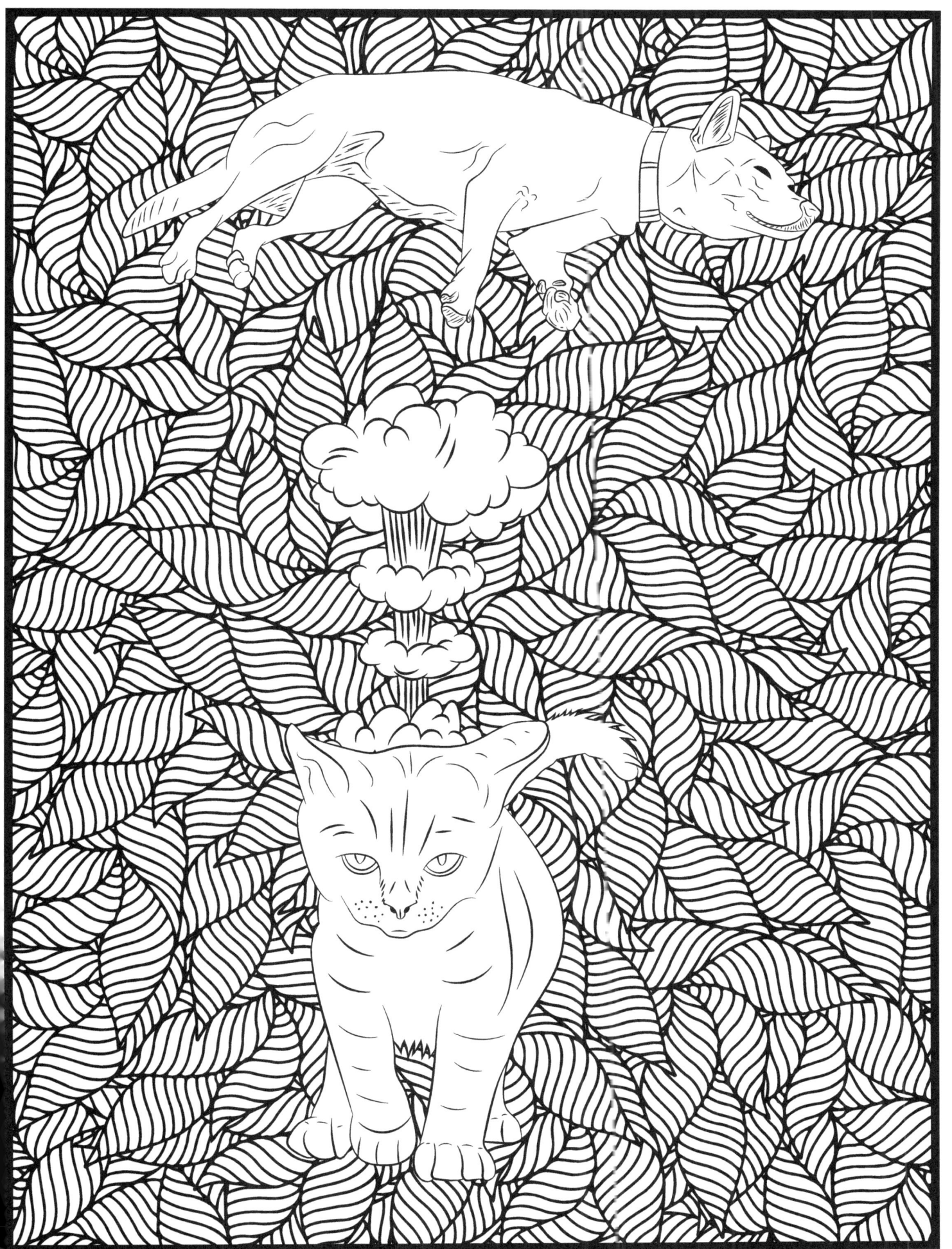

Colorful Swearing Dreams

Swear Word Coloring Book for Adults

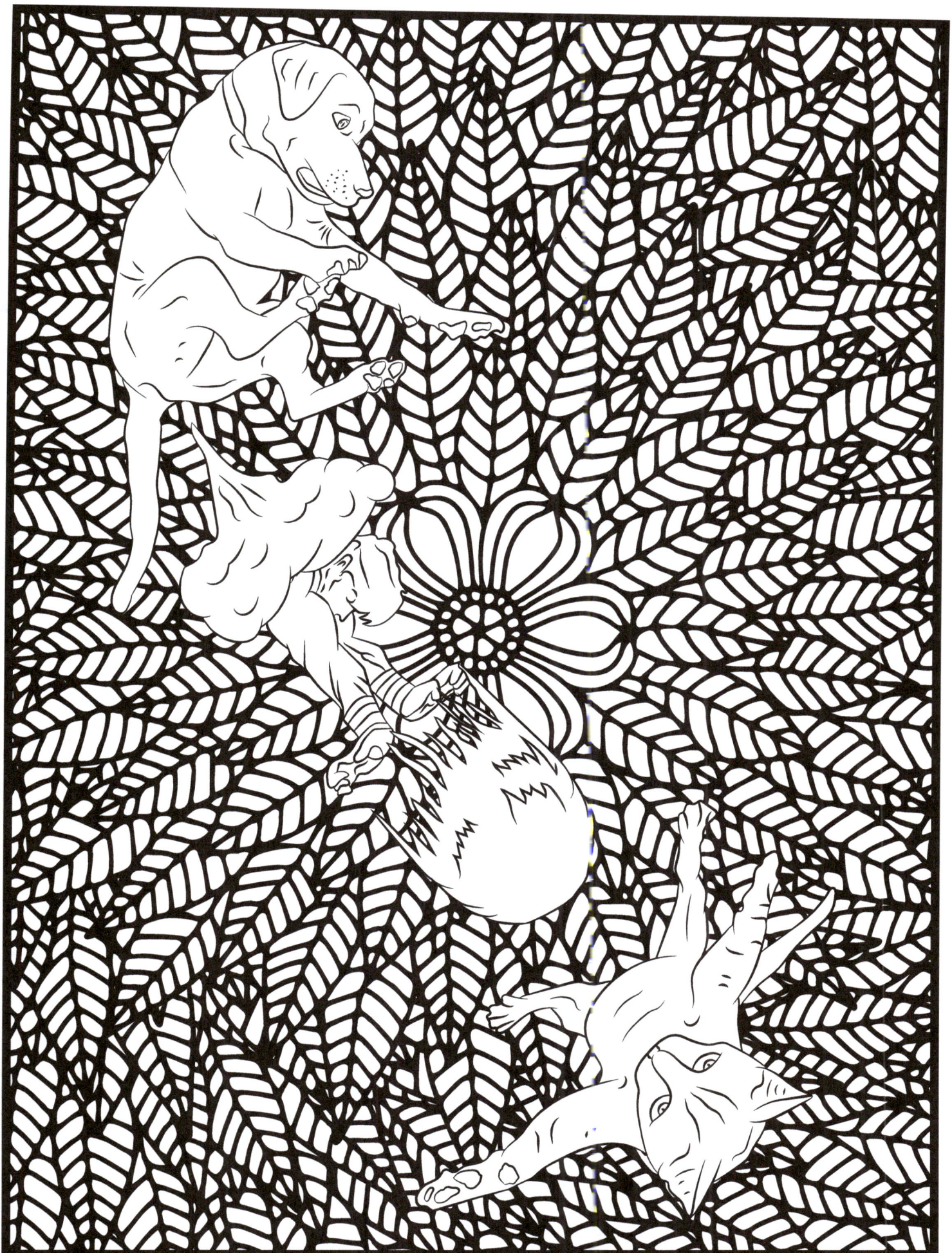

Colorful Swearing Dreams

Swear Word Coloring Book for Adults

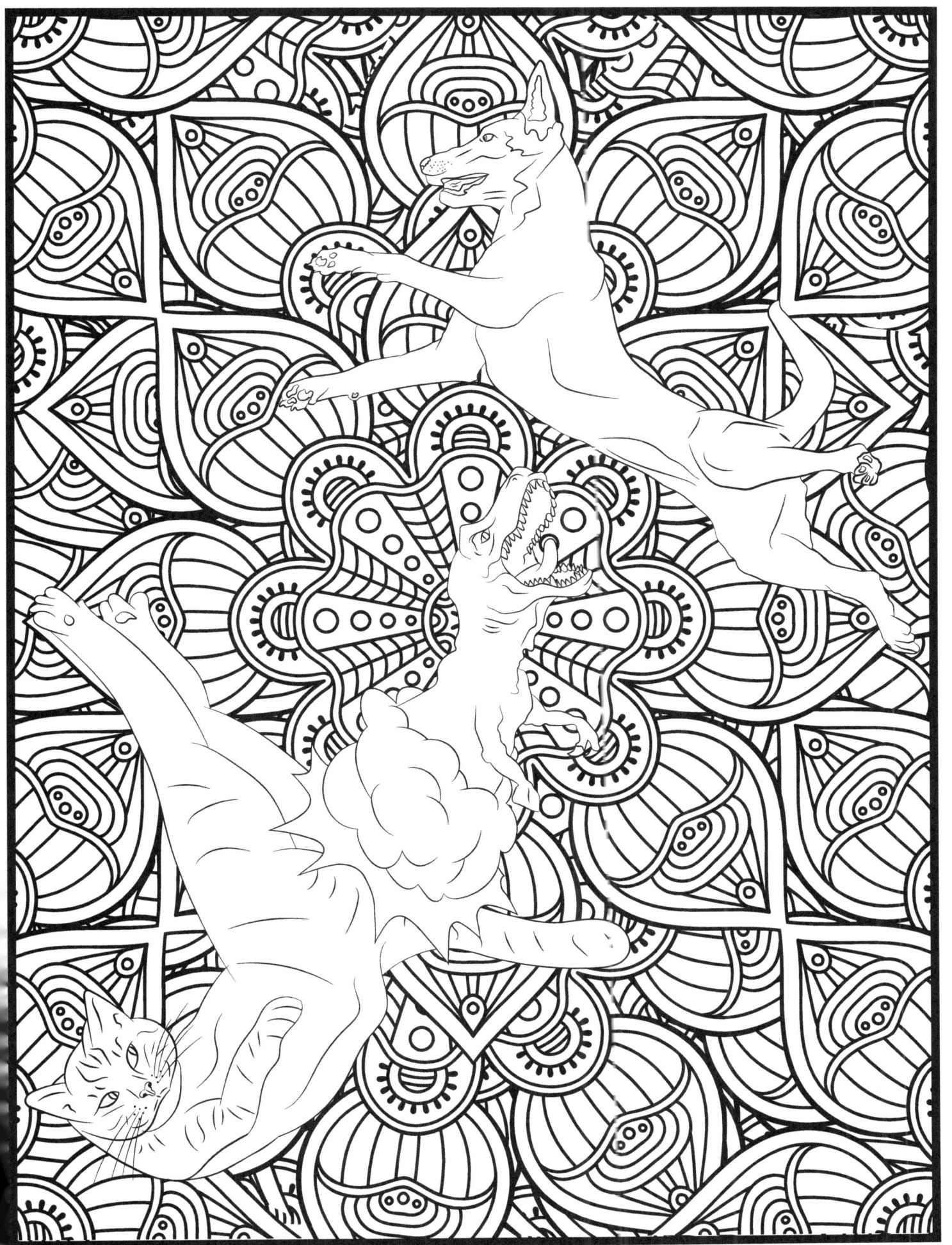

Colorful Swearing Dreams

Swear Word Coloring Book for Adults

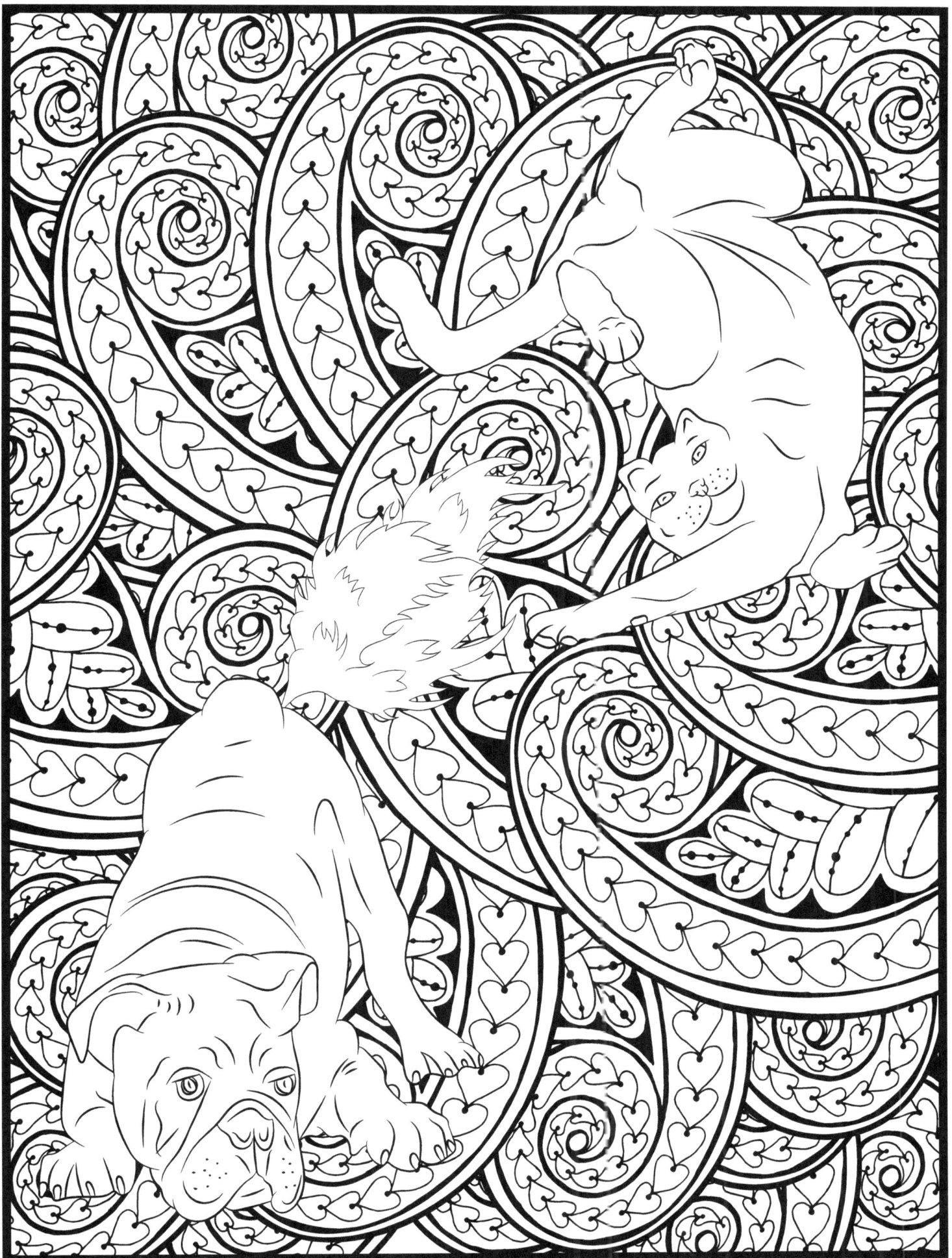

Colorful Swearing Dreams

Swear Word Coloring Book for Adults

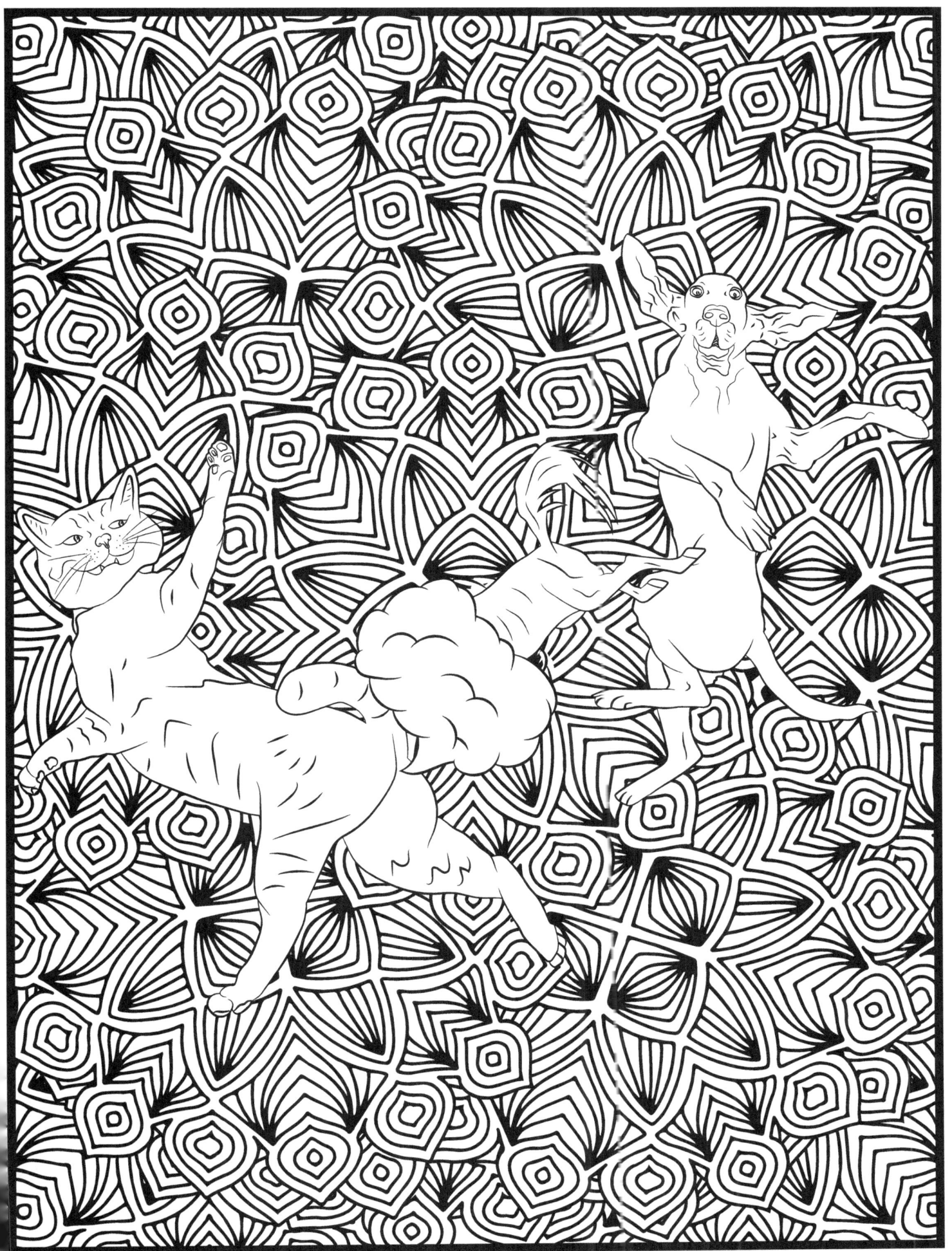

Colorful Swearing Dreams

Swear Word Coloring Book for Adults

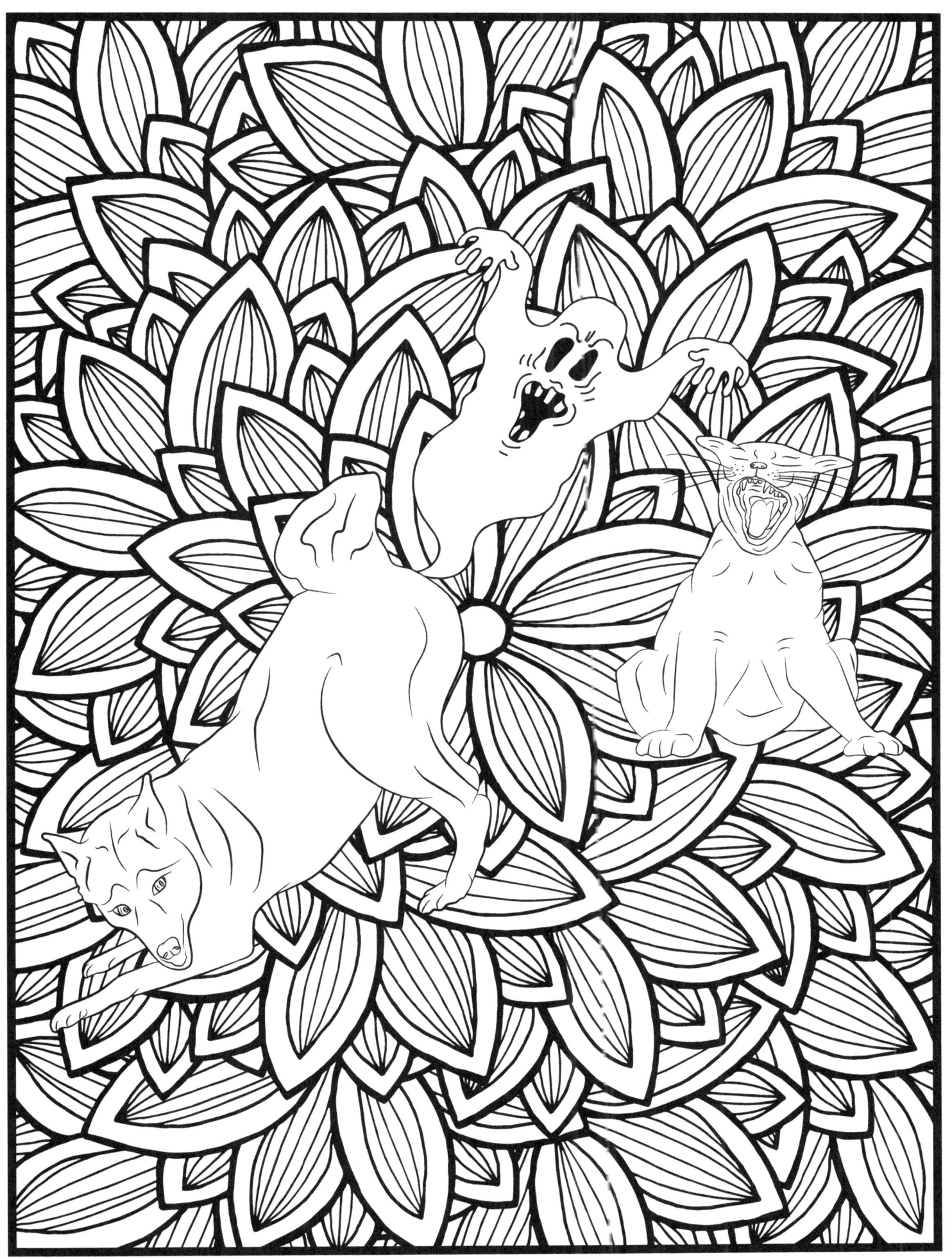

Colorful Swearing Dreams

Swear Word Coloring Book for Adults

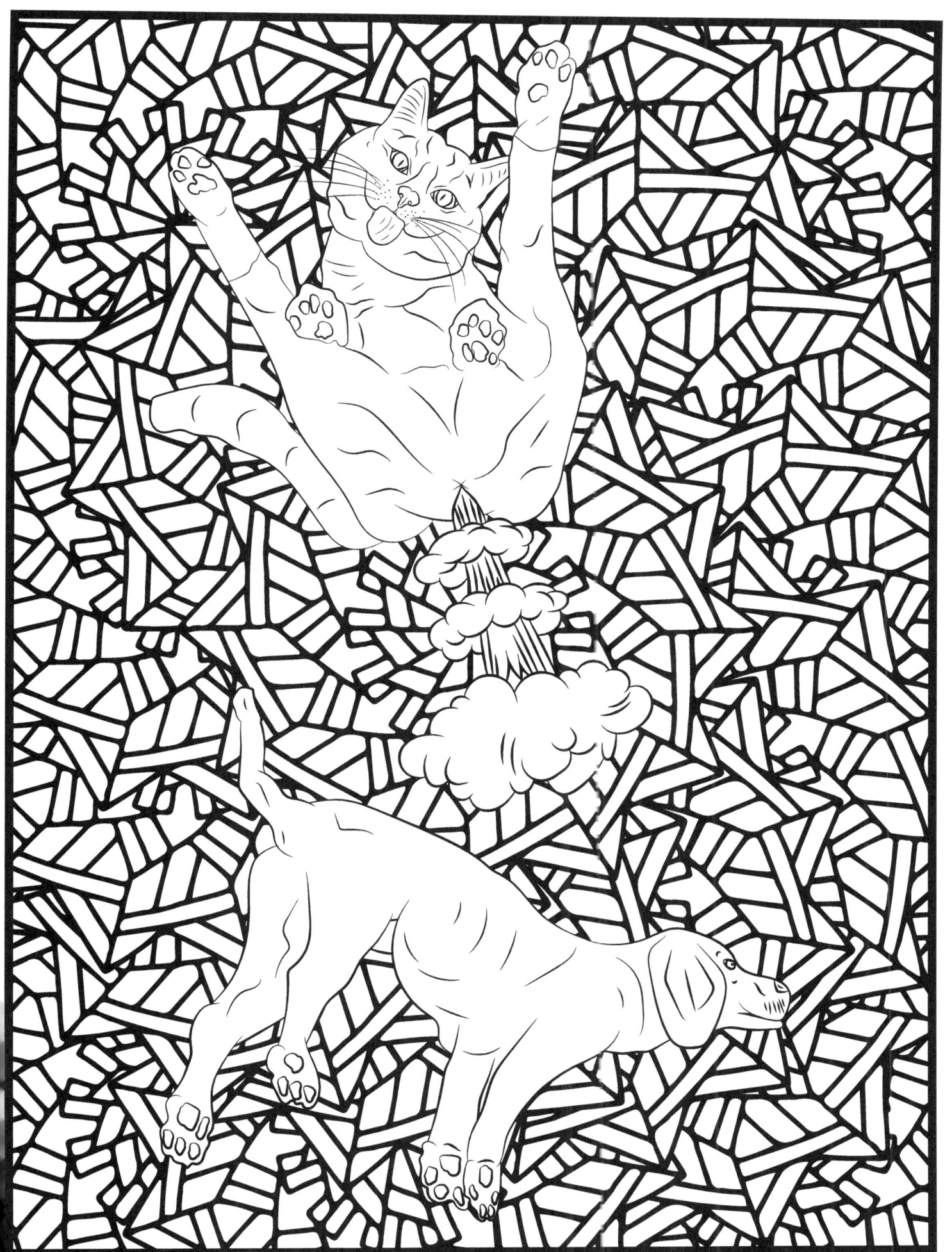

Colorful Swearing Dreams

Swear Word Coloring Book for Adults

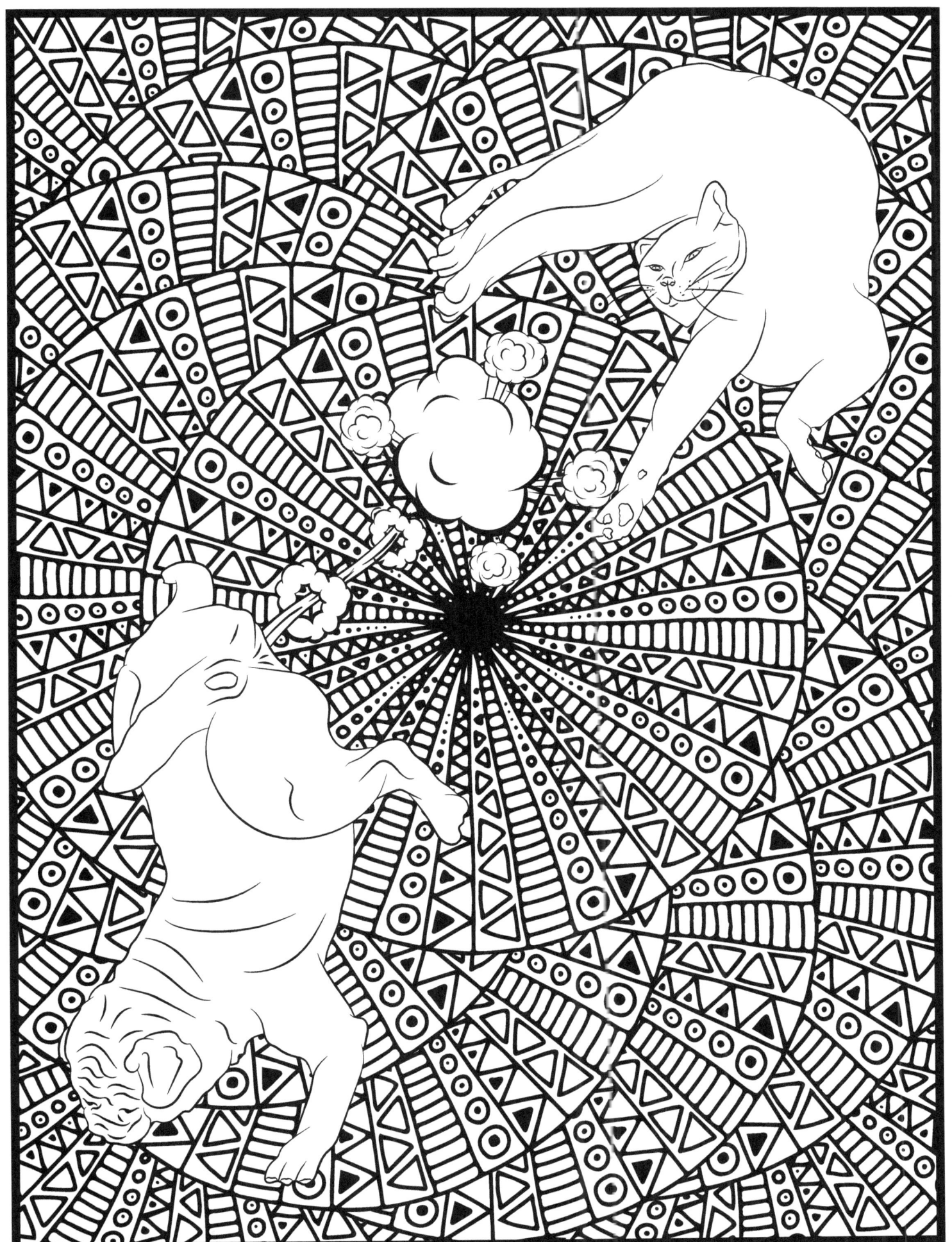

Colorful Swearing Dreams

Swear Word Coloring Book for Adults

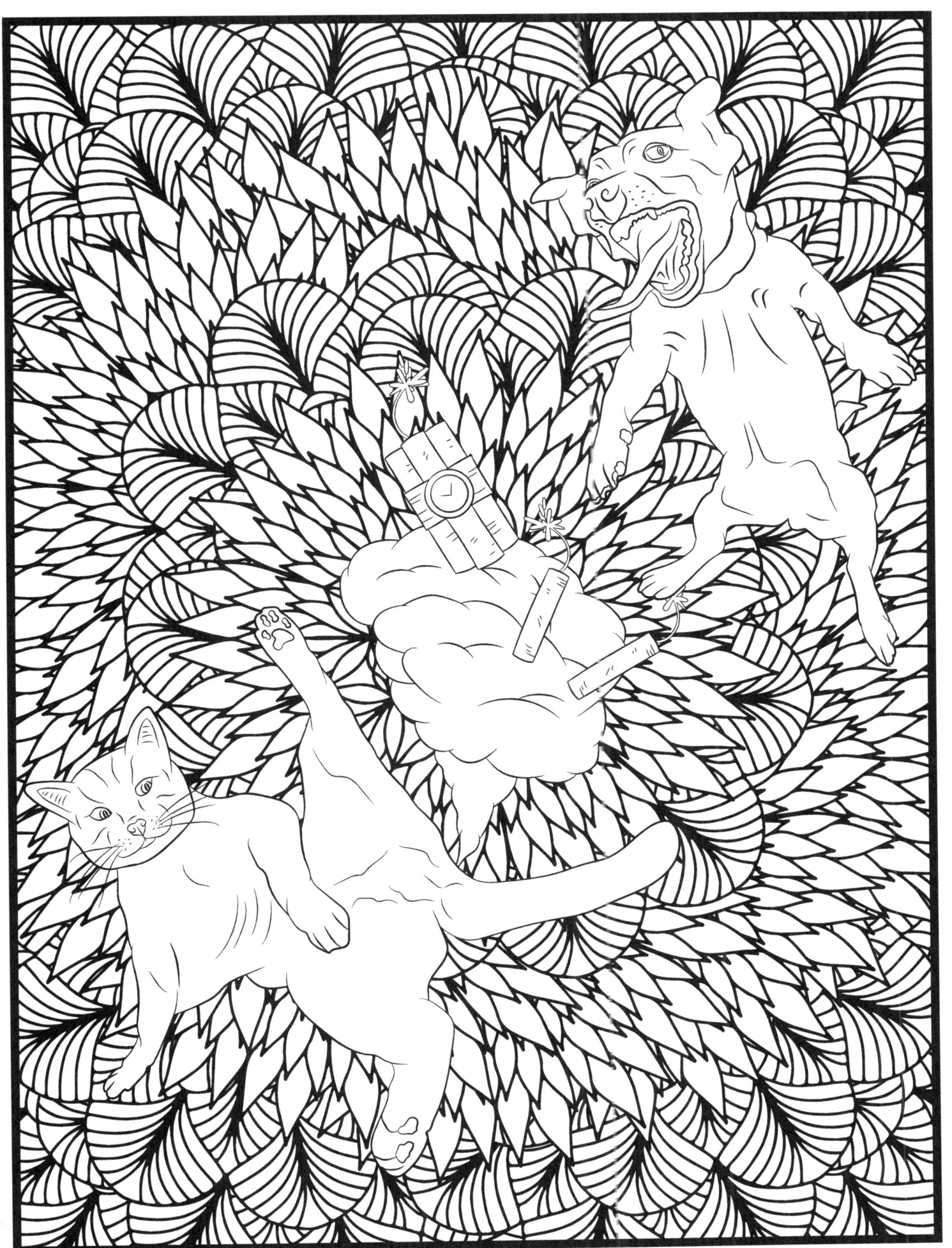

Colorful Swearing Dreams

Swear Word Coloring Book for Adults

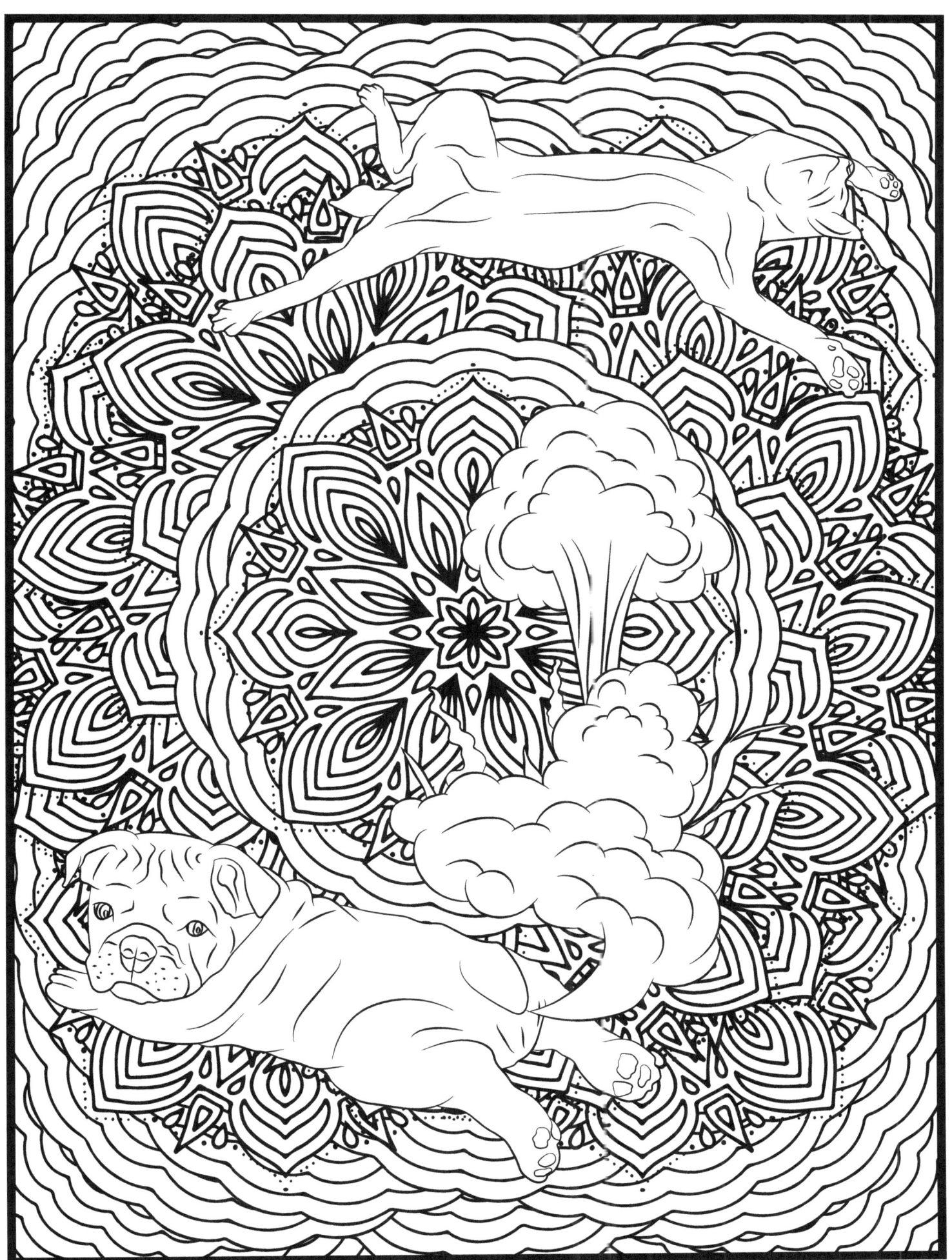

Colorful Swearing Dreams

Swear Word Coloring Book for Adults

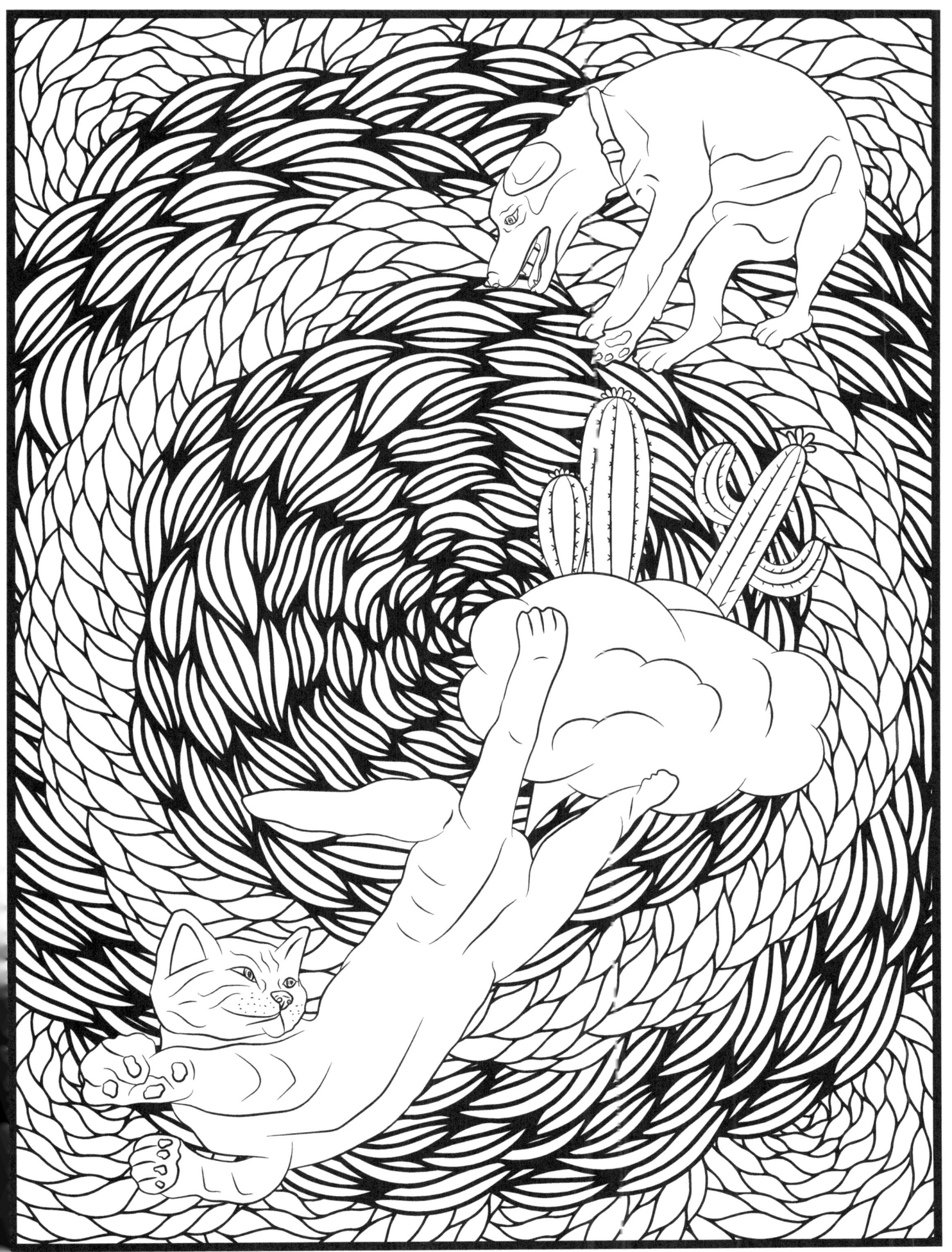

Colorful Swearing Dreams

Swear Word Coloring Book for Adults

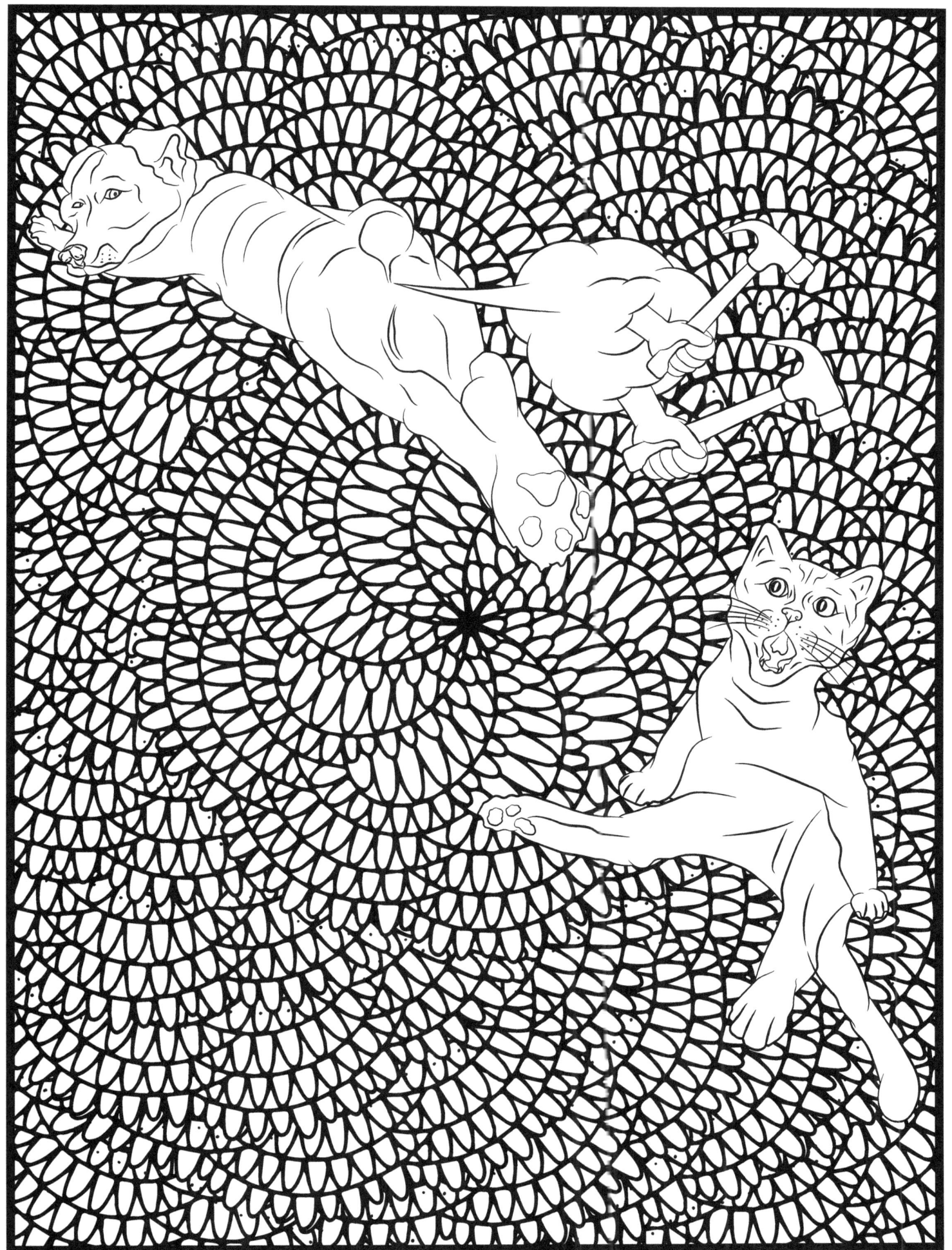

Colorful Swearing Dreams

Swear Word Coloring Book for Adults

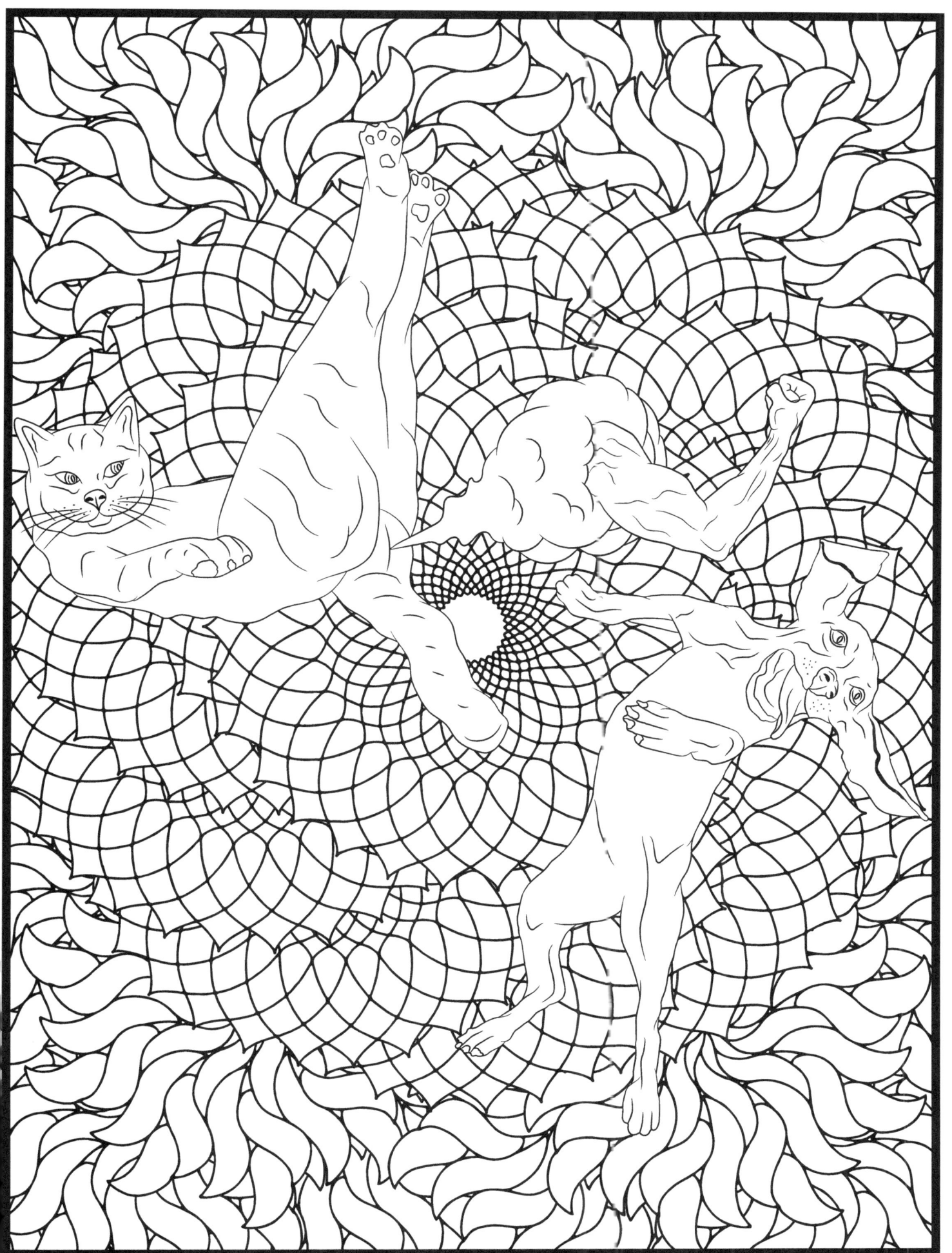

Colorful Swearing Dreams

Swear Word Coloring Book for Adults

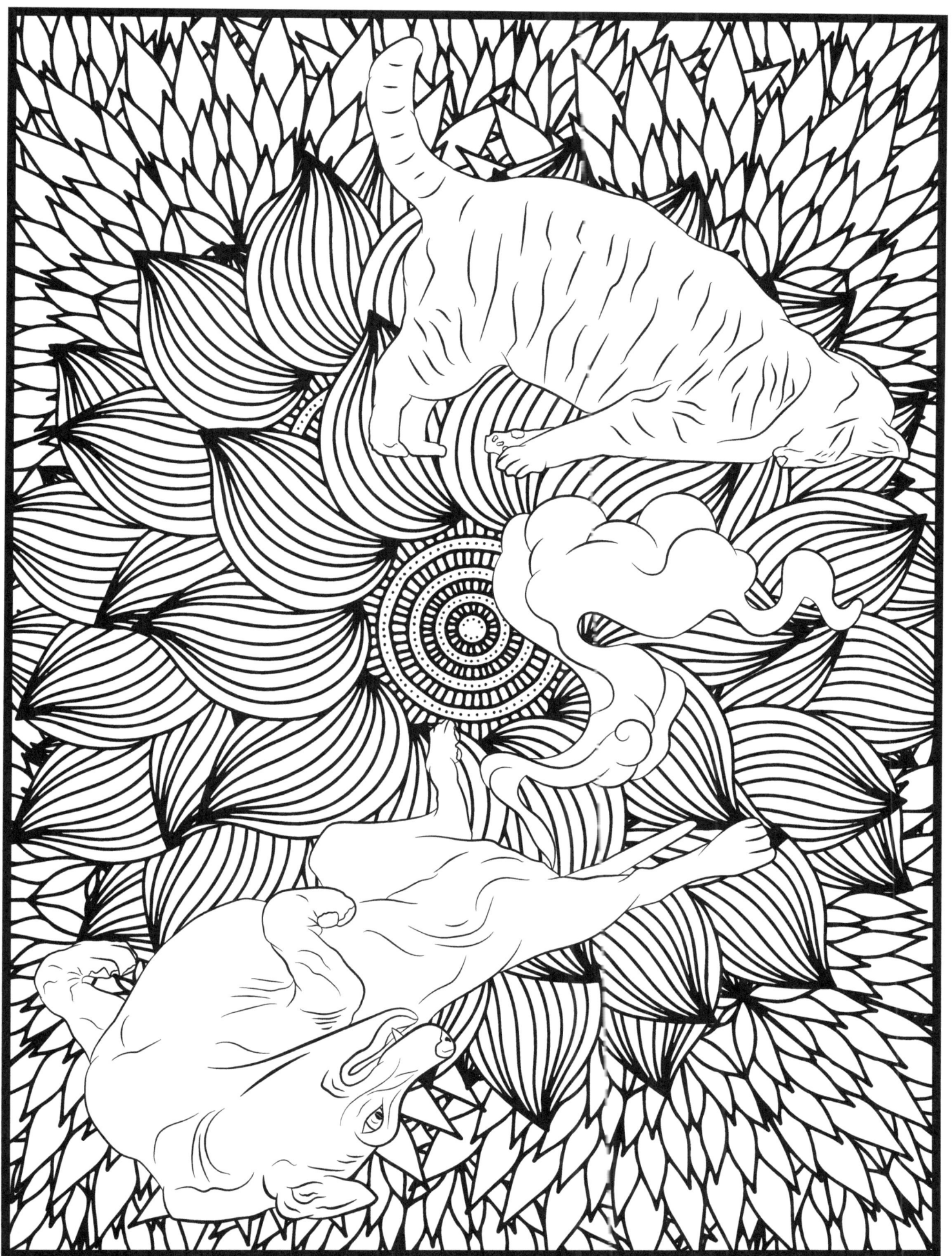

Colorful Swearing Dreams

Swear Word Coloring Book for Adults

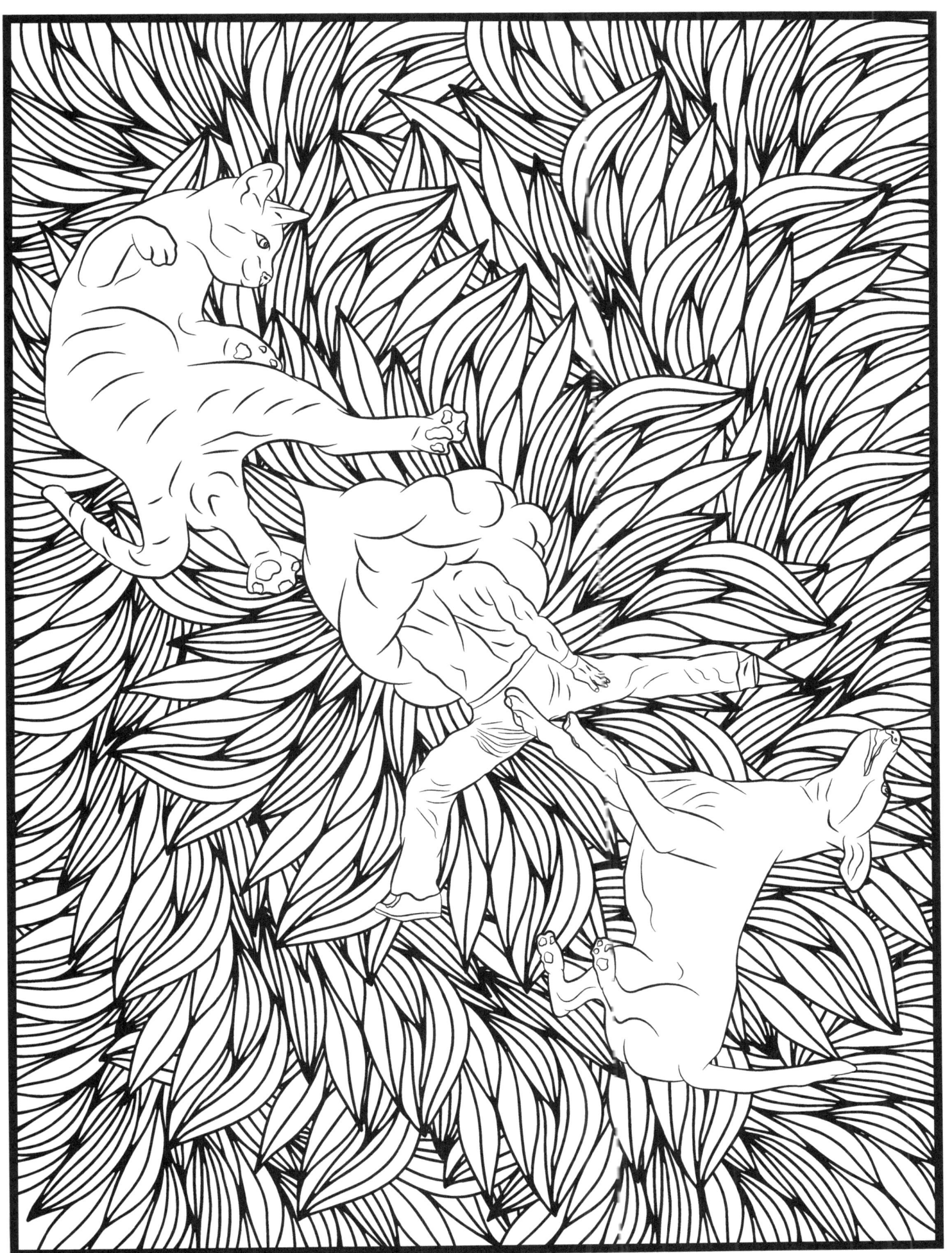

Colorful Sweaning Dreams

Sweet World Coloring Book for Adults

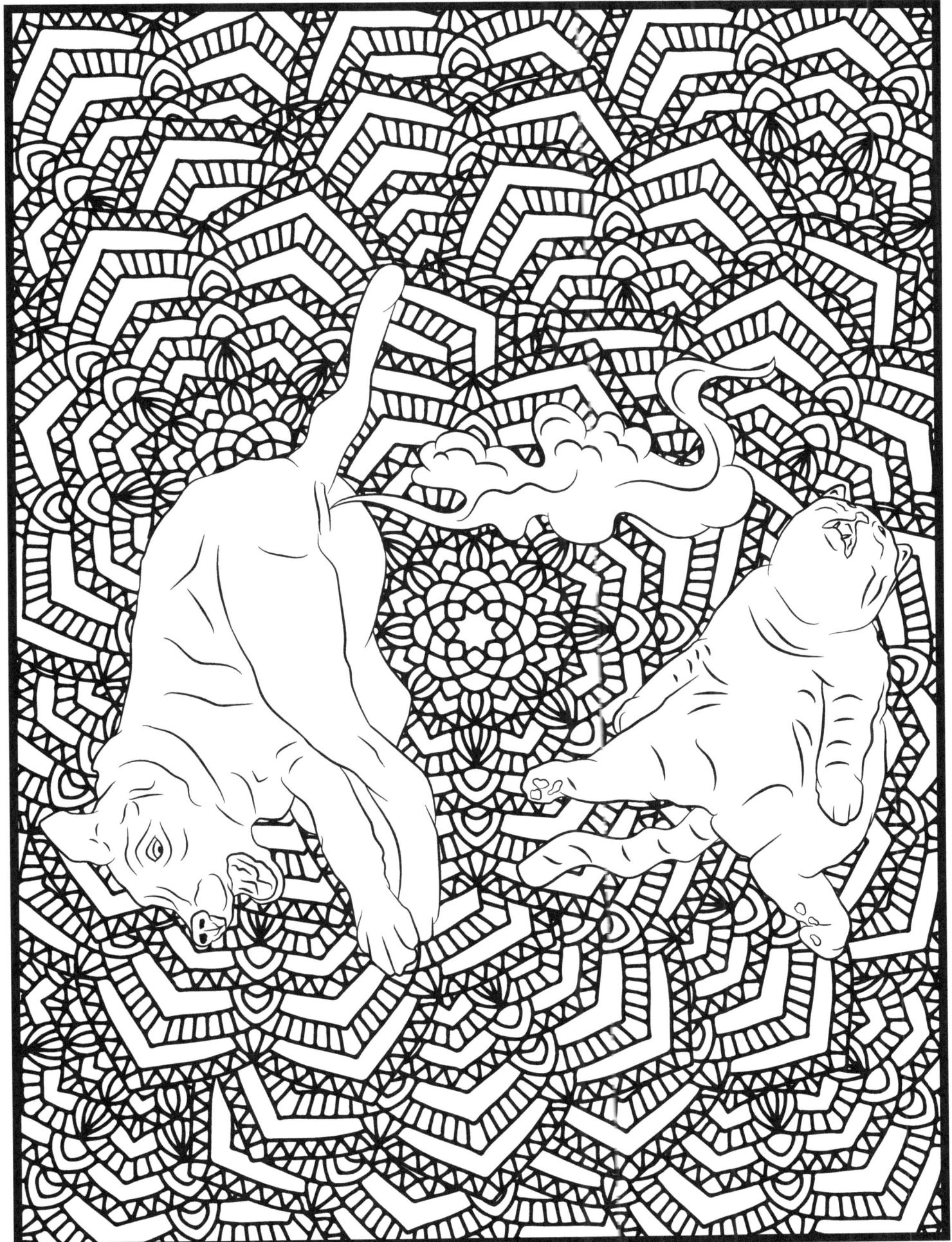

Colorful Swearing Dreams

Swear Word Coloring Book for Adults

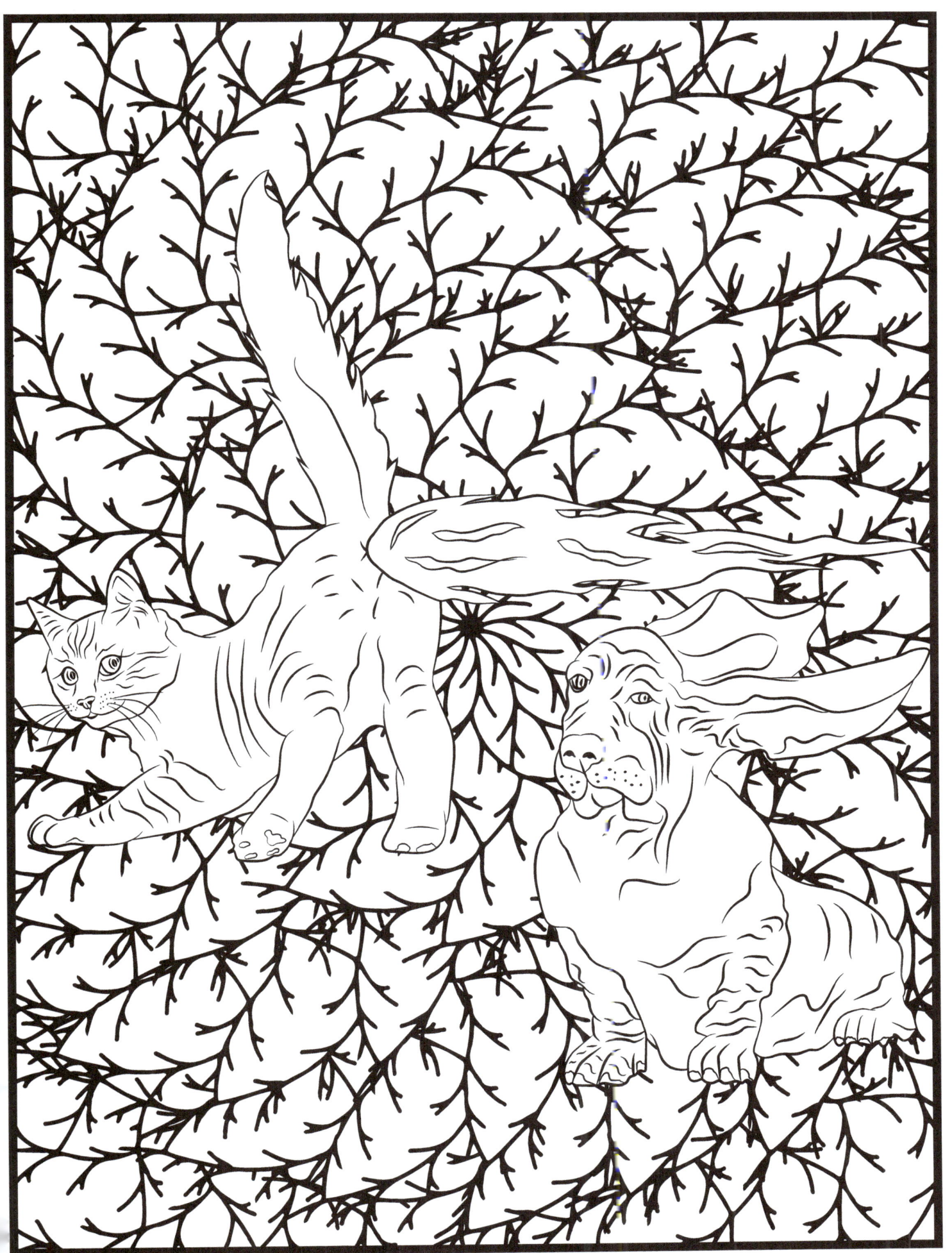

Colorful Swearing Dreams

Swear Word Coloring Book for Adults

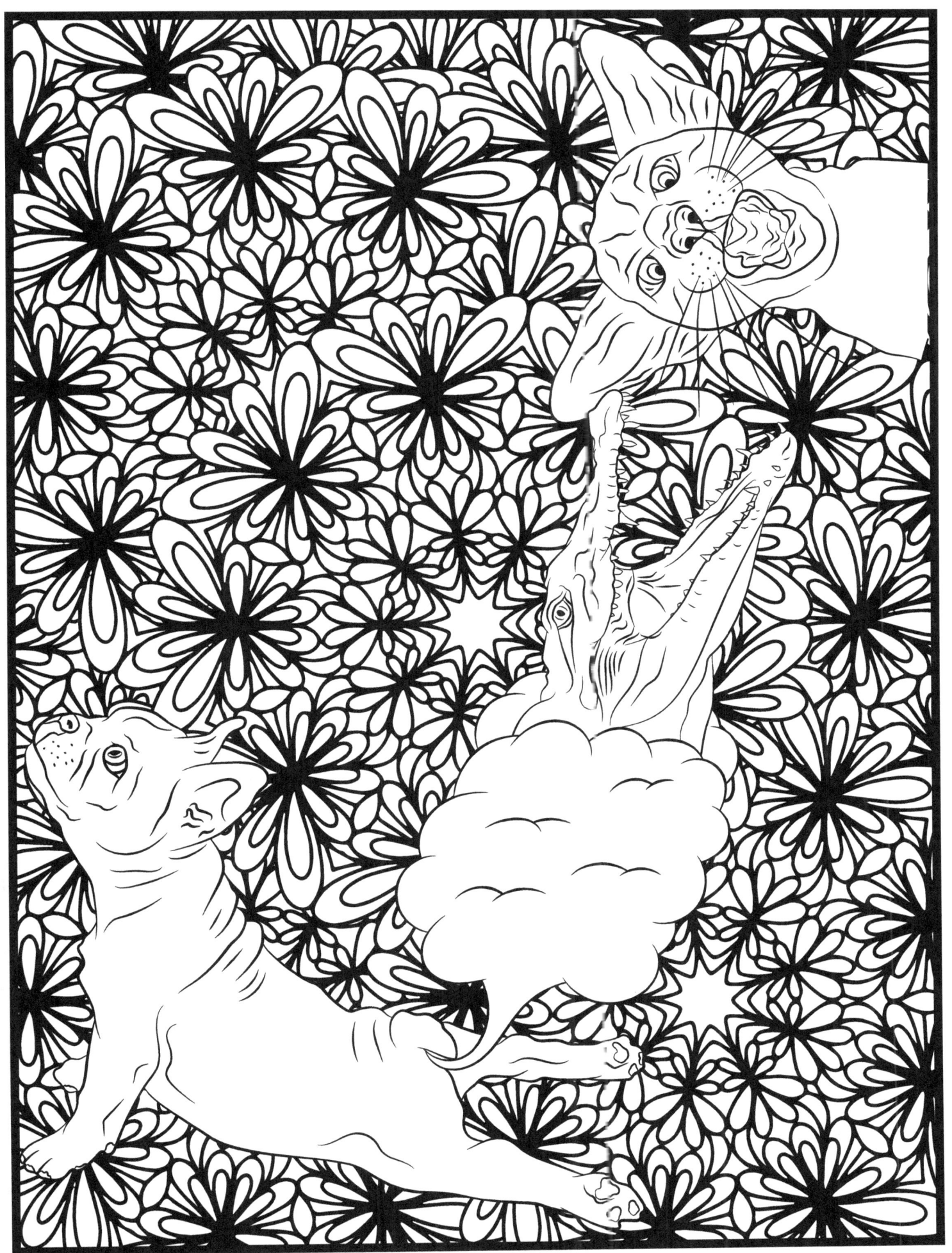

Colorful Sweaming Dreams

Sweet Land Coloring Book for Adults

Colorful Swearing Dreams

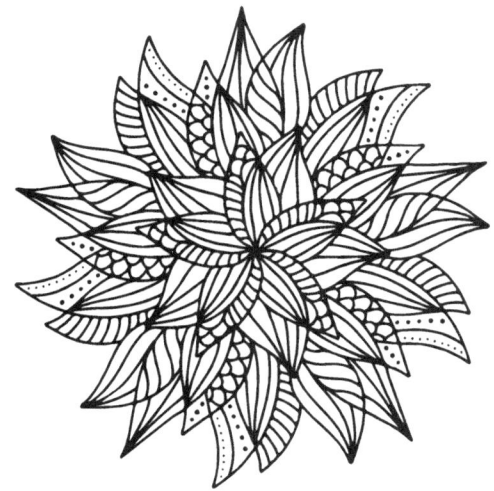

How is your stress level now?

Would you be kind enough to review our book?

Did the book allow you to put all the stress out of your mind, body and soul?
Hopefully you now feel fulfilled, relaxed and happy.

We sure put a lot of effort to provide you the best product possible that fits all your needs.

YOUR REVIEW is extremely valuable to us.
We don't see it as just a star rating, we read and study the feedbacks so we can consistently improve our products to shape them how you want them to be.

We take pride in making quality products for your satisfaction.

That is why, we would really appreciate if you can take few minutes of your time and leave us a review on our product's page.
That way, not only you will help other customers to make the right decision but you will also allow us to make other quality products that can make funny & unique gifts for your friends and family to just make them happy!

All Rights Reserved. Colorful Swearing Dreams

No part of this book may be reproduced, stored in a retrieval system, or transmitted in any form or by any means, electronic, mechanical, photocopying, recording, or otherwise, without the prior written permission of the author.

www.ingramcontent.com/pod-product-compliance
Lightning Source LLC
Chambersburg PA
CBHW060439220526
45465CB00008B/3204